Discovering Cultural Japan

Boye De Mente

PASSPORT BOOKS

Trade Imprint of National Textbook Company
Lincolnwood, Illinois U.S.A.

Contents

CHAPTER III

Nihonjin No Kao

Faces of the Japanese

CHAPTER IV

Nihon No Tanoshimi No Koto

The Joys of Japan

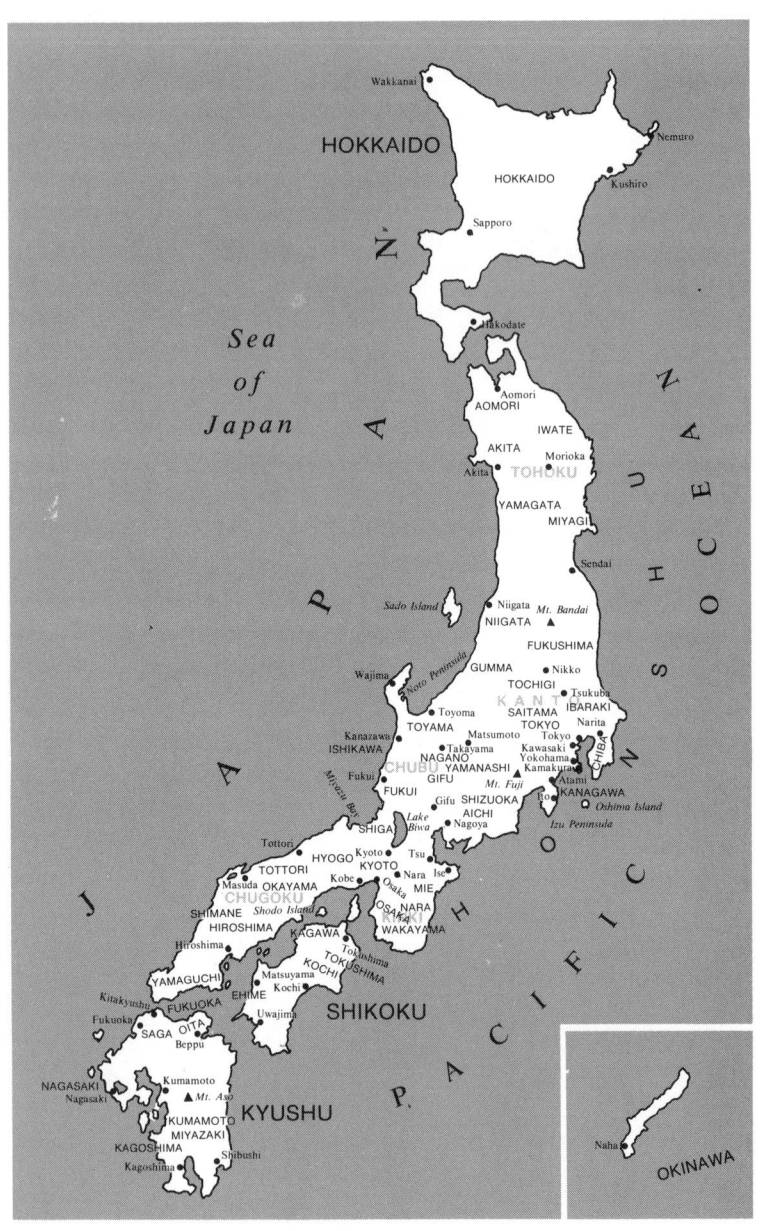

Japan in Profile

Location

Japan is located off the eastern coast of the Asian continent, beginning just below the Russian-held island of Sakhalin (which adjoins Siberia) and stretching in a south and southwesterly direction, arc-fashion, from 45 degrees north latitude to 20 degrees north latitude. From tip to tip, the island chain is 3,800 kilometers long. At its westernmost point, Japan is only a little more than 100 miles from Korea on the Asian mainland.

If superimposed over a map of the eastern coast of the U.S., Japan would stretch from Bangor, Maine, to Jacksonville, Florida—and have about the same kind of climate.

Tokyo is 35 degrees north of the equator, and therefore on approximately the same latitude as Tehran, Athens, Norfolk, and San Francisco.

Landmass

Japan is made up of four relatively large islands, several dozen medium-sized ones and thousands of tiny islets, with a total landmass of 377,765 square kilometers (approximately 142,000 square miles), which makes it about fifty percent larger than the United Kingdom, a little larger than Norway and Italy, but only one-twenty-fifth the size of the U.S.

Seventy-one percent of Japan is made up of mountains that are mostly uninhabitable. The remaining twenty-nine percent consists of basins and plains.

Population

Japan's population is rapidly approaching the 123-million mark, or around half that of the United States. Approximately twenty-nine million of this number live in Metropolitan Tokyo and the surrounding suburban subcenters, and it is predicted that by the year 2000 this figure will balloon to 34.5 million. Over twenty-two million Japanese live in the Osaka-Kobe-Kyoto area. Since over seventy percent of Japan is mountainous and uninhabited, the total population lives on a land-area that is about the size of some of the larger counties in the American states of Texas, New Mexico, and Arizona.

Japan's population density is 325 persons per square kilometer, compared to 25 in the United States, 110 in China, 353 in the Netherlands, and 672 in Bangladesh.

Government

Japan has a democratic form of government similar to that of England and the United States, with three branches—the legislative, executive, and judicial. The chief executive officer is the prime minister, who is assisted by twenty cabinet ministers. The Diet (similar to Congress and Parliament) is made up of the House of Representatives (511 members) and the House of Councilors (252 members). The Cabinet can dissolve the Diet, and the House of Representatives can pass a motion of nonconfidence in the Cabinet, requiring the appointment of new ministers.

Japan's forty-seven prefectures are administered by governors and assemblies directly elected by residents of the prefectures. There are village, town, and city governments under the prefectural governments.

The judicial system consists of the supreme court, high courts, district courts, family courts, and summary courts.

The emperor of Japan is the symbol of the state but has no powers related to the government. His duties are very much like those of the king or queen of England.

Historical Note

The founding of Japan as a nation is generally given as B.C. 660, when uncorroborated history says the first emperor, Jimmu, was enthroned in what is now Nara Prefecture near Kyoto. Historical records in Korea and China indicate that the Yamato family established itself as the supreme political and military power in Japan, centered in the Nara area, sometime between 200 and 300 A.D. (Yamato was an early name for Japan.) During these centuries, the emperor was both the religious and secular leader of the country.

The primary social organization at that time was the family-related clan, with leadership hereditary. Each of the clan leaders maintained hegemony in their own territories, usually with the advice and consent of the imperial court. The bulk of the people were fishermen, farmers, and hunters.

Contact with nearby Korea and China became common between the third and seventh centuries A.D., resulting in an influx of culture from these two highly advanced civilizations. Architecture, Buddhism, Confucianism, the ideographic system of writing, city planning, ceramic making, lacquering, landscaping, tea, court manners, and apparel styles were just some of the hundreds of concepts, products, and skills that flowed into Japan from the Asian mainland during these long generations.

After some four centuries of absorbing massive amounts of Korean and Chinese culture, the Japanese virtually broke off contact with the mainland and spent the next several hundred years synthesizing and Japanizing the imported technologies and philosophies. The arts, crafts, and literature flourished. Thousands of temples and shrines were built. A road system was extended throughout the country. A new, large capital city was built and named Kyoto.

The imperial family grew into many branches. The imperial court became large and ritualized, with ceremonial pomp and pageantry that rivaled that of the Chinese emperors and Korean kings. Members of the royal families dressed in rich, colorful attire, and spent most of their time in religious, cultural, and recreational pursuits.

As the number of imperial princes and their families grew, the emperor began dispatching some of them to outlying areas as administrators of provincial domains. As the generations passed, these positions became hereditary. The domains became the fiefs of the ruling families, which gradually developed into large clans.

These provincial clan lords imitated the imperial court, with their own religious and political rituals, as well as cultural activities. Life for the privileged classes became highly refined and sophisticated. The sons and daughters of the clan lords enjoyed the titles and the prerogatives of princes and princesses.

Thus it came about that a small minority made up of the imperial family and its branches and the provincial clan lords and ladies lived a life of privileged luxury, supported by the labor of peasant farmers and plebeian craftsmen who had few legal rights and for the most part survived at a subsistence level.

The ties binding the clans to the imperial government continued to loosen. The larger and richer clan lords virtually became independent rulers, with their own armies, and began vying for supreme power. In the late 1100s warfare broke out between the largest of the clans. In 1192 the famous Minamoto clan, under the leadership of Yoritomo Minamoto, defeated the Heike clan and became the primary power in the country. Yoritomo forced the then weak imperial court to appoint him *shogun* (generalissimo), which in effect made him the military dictator of Japan.

This form of government was to endure in Japan until the latter part of the nineteenth century, with a number of relatively long shogunate dynasties succeeding each other after prolonged wars in which competing clans would challenge the power of the shogun, eventually win out, and set up their own shogunate.

The professional warriors maintained by the shogunate and the two hundred-plus provincial fiefs that developed under the new system of government came to be known as *samurai* (sah-muu-rie), from the word, *saburai* (sah-buu-rie), meaning "to guard." The profession of samurai became hereditary, and the samurai families gradually emerged as a new elite, privileged class that was to administer the laws and rules of the clan governments as well as the shogunate until modern times.

By the early 1500s, the ruling Ashikaga shogunate had become so smitten by the cultural refinements of Kyoto that it began to lose military control of the country. Ambitious clan lords in the larger and richer fiefs began contesting for power. In the mid-1500s, Nobunaga Oda emerged as the undisputed military ruler, but before he could consolidate his power and form a new shogunate, he was assassinated. His most capable general, Hideyoshi Toyotomi, who began life as an incorrigible runaway peasant boy and the mascot of a robber gang, quickly defeated Oda's enemies. Because of his lowly origins, there was too much opposition to Hideyoshi having himself named shogun, so he settled for the title of prime minister.

Hideyoshi ruled Japan with an iron hand, and became a patron of the arts and a builder on a massive scale. Among his projects was the great Osaka Castle, which still may be seen today. With his power in Japan absolute and his rebuilding of the nation complete, Hideyoshi sent a huge army to invade and conquer Korea, and then proceed on to China, but he became ill and the army was recalled short of victory. Hideyoshi died before the army could return to Japan.

Ieyasu Tokugawa, Hideyoshi's most ambitious and talented ally, quickly moved to consolidate power in his own hands. After a series of battles against other lords, Ieyasu emerged the winner, and in 1603 established the Tokugawa Shogunate, which was to be Japan's last shogunate dynasty.

Ieyasu moved his headquarters to the small fishing village of Edo at the head of Edo Bay, greatly enlarged a castle that had been built there in the 1400s as a frontier outpost, and set about restructuring the political divisions of the country. Clan lords who had supported him were reconfirmed in their positions and their relations with the new shogunate government. Those who had opposed him were subject to a variety of restrictions designed to keep them in line.

One final battle in 1613 eliminated the family and loyal allies of Hideyoshi Toyotomi, who resented Ieyasu's seizure of power and had continuously intrigued against him since Hideyoshi's death.

The first Westerners had arrived in Japan in 1543, when

a storm blew a Chinese junk off course and it landed on the tiny island of Tanega, twenty miles off the coast of Kyushu, south of the city of Kagoshima. Among the passengers on the ship were three Dutch traders, who had with them guns, tobacco, and syphilis—all three of which were left on the island when they resumed their voyage to Macau.

News of the discovery of a highly civilized island nation off the coast of Korea and China spread rapidly among Europeans in Southeast Asia, and just six years later the first Western missionary, a Jesuit priest named Xavier, arrived in Japan and traded the local clan lords guns and other Western products for permission to preach the Christian religion. Xavier was followed by other missionaries and by traders. Within a few decades there were several hundred foreigners resident in Japan, and many thousands of Japanese had been converted to Christianity.

Word of the warlike nature of the Europeans and their penchant for colonizing less developed countries began to worry Nobunaga Oda. The missionaries in Japan had begun to intrigue against each other, and to favor one clan lord over another with their gifts of guns and other Western things. Nobunaga ordered all missionaries to leave and outlawed the teaching and practice of Christianity. Some missionaries who refused to leave were put to death but the edict was not always enforced.

During the reign of Hideyoshi Toyotomi from 1583 to 1598, actions against missionaries and Japanese Christians were renewed, and many were killed, but once again internal political events distracted Hideyoshi's attention away from the foreigners. Will Adams, the Englishman who was the role model for the pilot in Robert Clavel's famous novel and TV extravaganza *Shogun*, was blown ashore in Japan in 1600, and subsequently became a friend and advisor to Ieyasu Tokugawa, who was to establish the Tokugawa shogunate in 1603.

Problems with missionaries and foreigners continued

following Ieyasu's retirement and death in 1616. Finally, Ieyasu's grandson, Iemitsu, closed Japan off from the rest of the world in 1637, ordering all foreigners out of the country and decreeing the death sentence for anyone, including Japanese who happened to be abroad at that time, who attempted to enter Japan.

The only exception to this law was a small Dutch-operated trading post on a man-made island called *Deshima* (day-she-mah) in Nagasaki harbor. The Dutch were allowed to keep a few traders there and to bring in one ship a year for the exchange of goods. Chinese traders were also allowed limited access to Japan through the post.

This single tiny window to the outside world was the only official contact Japan was to have with the West until the 1850s, when America's Commodore Perry arrived with his squadron of black warships and delivered an ultimatum to the aging Tokugawa shogunate to open Japan to foreign trade, or else.

In the intervening years of the Tokugawa Period, Edo had grown into one of the largest cities on earth. Japanese culture had flourished and evolved into one of the world's most distinctive civilizations. But the country was still a feudalistic society of lords, ladies, sword-carrying warriors, peasants, and plebeians, such as had not been seen in Europe and the U.S. for many generations.

Opening Japan to the outside world resulted in the fall of the Tokugawa shogunate, the formation of a parliamentary type of government, and the rapid industrialization and modernization of the country. Victorious in a war against China in 1895 and against Russia in 1904–1905, the Japanese quickly emerged on the international scene as a formidable people—highly disciplined and educated, and determined to catch up with and surpass the West at its own game of industrial and military hegemony.

These ultranationalistic motives led the Japanese to the

debacle of World War II, which, as destructive and as tragic as it was, opened the way for genuine democracy and individual freedom in Japan, and loosed a torrent of Japanese talent and ambition that has propelled them into the front ranks of the world's peoples.

The Addressing System in Japan

Most streets in Japan are not named, and the addressing system has nothing to do with streets. Instead it is based on areas that differ in shape and size. Homes and buildings within these areas are numbered, but because of the irregular shapes of the areas, the numbers may not be in sequence on the same street-front for more than a hundred yards or so, and then the sequence continues somewhere behind that line of buildings. There may be fifty or more buildings jammed together in one area that is the equivalent of three or four square blocks, so there would be several "lines," often not straight, of sequential numbers.

Larger cities in Japan are divided into wards *(ku)*, which are further divided into smaller areas with a variety of names such as Nihonbashi, Aoyama, Sakamachi, etc., which in turn may or may not be divided into areas called *chome* (choe-may) that are subdivided into yet smaller sections called *banchi* (bahn-chee). A typical address in Tokyo is: Tokyo, Shibuya Ward, 6 chome, 1-28 banchi. This means the twenty-eighth building in banchi number one, which is part of the sixth chome in Shibuya. Another version of a Tokyo address is: Chiyoda Ward, Kojimachi, 4 chome, 3-10 banchi—the tenth building in banchi number three, in the fourth chome in the area known as Kojimachi, which is one of dozens of named areas in Chiyoda Ward.

If this sounds complicated, it is. The secret of finding addresses in Tokyo and in Japan in general is to determine

their location in relation to some well-known transportation terminal or station, intersection, park, shrine, major
building, or some other landmark. Once you are in the
vicinity of the landmark you begin to look for the name and
number of the area on small plaques posted on telephone
or other poles along the street or on the fronts of buildings.
There is no particular uniformity of size or style for address signs so it is often necessary to search for them. Many
homes and buildings, especially larger office buildings and
government buildings, do not have address signs posted
anywhere. If you don't know the name of the building you
are looking for you have to ask someone—often someone
who works in the building—if that is the proper building or
address.

Best thing to do before you start out for a new address is
have someone draw a detailed location map for you (by
calling the address concerned and getting specific guidelines, if necessary). Or, if you are going by taxi, to have the
address and location written out in Japanese to hand to the
driver. Hotel and inn staffs in Japan are old hands at this
important service.

Introduction

Putting the Fun Back into Travel

For several decades the international travel industry has concentrated much of its effort and money on taking the unfamiliar—and consequently much of the adventure and pleasure—out of traveling abroad.

If this sounds like a contradiction, you're right. It is. Everyone knows that going abroad as a tourist is supposed to be adventurous and fun as well as educational.

Of course, the travel industry is not deliberately being contrary or uncaring. The principle it has been following is to provide travelers with the kind and quality of accommodations and food they are used to at home—if not better. Along with this just-like-home service come guides, interpreters, and others who look after the needs and desires of travelers to the extent that about all the travelers have to do is feed and bathe themselves and do their own shopping (although *all* of *these* services are also available to the traveler who wants to take advantage of them).

The unfortunate thing, of course, is that this sanitized and homogenized system isolates the traveler from the personal experiences that make traveling worthwhile and memorable. Wrapped in the womb of the system from beginning to end, the traveler becomes little more than an arm's-length observer.

Because of this system, many travelers make no effort to learn anything about the country they are going to visit. Their trip abroad thus becomes little more than a physical interlude spent mostly on planes and buses and in hotels, with a series of images they glimpse in passing. One might be better off watching a good travel video at home. It's much cheaper and there is no jet lag.

But if you have the means, the time, and the imagination to travel abroad, you owe it to yourself to get as much as possible out of the trip.

It is my contention that Japan is one of the greatest travel experiences in the world today for anyone who is willing to learn a little about the country and expose himself or herself to its pleasures.

The Japanese are exceedingly courteous, friendly, and hospitable (with none of the arrogance or snobbery that is frequently encountered in some countries I could name). They routinely go beyond expectations in their efforts to help visitors enjoy their country.

Japan is rich in natural scenery. Great expanses of the country are so gorgeous they captivate the senses and the spirit.

Japanese cuisine offers an extensive variety of dishes of gourmet quality that may be hard to pronounce and have a different look, but are nevertheless delicious and nutritious, and are worth adding to your daily diet.

The traditional lifestyle of the Japanese offers the visitor an opportunity for new experiences that are the achievements of a highly sophisticated, distinctive culture that has been continuous for over two thousand years.

The aesthetic and metaphysical arts of Japan are based on classic, universal principles that please the mind and nurture the spirit—and are readily available to the visitor who has even a little advance knowledge and the smallest amount of energy and interest.

This book is designed to provide you with the historical and cultural perspective, the insights and the knowledge you need to intellectually, emotionally, and physically cross the cultural barriers into the inner circle of Japanese life and savor it to the fullest extent possible.

There are, in fact, two Japans. One is the product of modern industry and is therefore similar to other highly industrialized countries. The other is the Japan of the past—the "Traditional Japan" that traces its beginnings back more than twenty-five hundred years. It is this traditional world that makes Japan a unique experience for the visitor from abroad. The visitor is able to move freely back and forth between the two ways of life, enjoying the best of both just as the Japanese do.

My own love affair with Japan began when I was twenty years old, and my ardor has increased with the years. There have been ups and downs, of course, as in any passionate relationship, but as a mistress Japan is incomparable. No matter how many loves may come afterward, none ever entirely replaces her.

I am not alone.

Almost everyone who has spent more than a few days in Japan has succumbed to some degree to its fascination. And, like myself, most who spend any considerable time there find their lives permanently changed.

What is this spell that Japan casts upon even the most jaded traveler? What is it, exactly, that makes Japan so different, so much of an "out of this world" experience? The answer to this question is found in the distinctive attitudes and etiquette of the Japanese and in the style of living they developed during their long history.

In its idealized form, this style of living, known as *The Japanese Way,* came close to fulfilling the sensual, intellectual, and spiritual needs of man. The primary goal of the system was harmony—among men and between men and nature. The lifestyle included the practicing of a highly refined system of manners, humility, hospitality, generosity, and instinctive unselfishness.

The Japanese Way also included an extraordinarily well-developed sense of aesthetic taste in matters relating to architecture, interior decoration, handicrafts, and even in the serving of food. There were numerous contemplative exercises designed to contribute to mental and spiritual maturity. There was also a relaxed, natural attitude toward sensual pleasures.

This unique mode of living is still maintained by vast numbers of Japanese, although the majority now follow the old traditional way only on a part-time basis. In the cities it is to be found in numerous private homes, in purely Japanese-style restaurants, in inns, and in thousands of temples and shrines. It is still the rule rather than the exception in a majority of rural homes; and the farther one gets from the great urban areas, the more traditional becomes the style of living.

For the growing number of urban Japanese who now live more or less Western-style, the traditional-style inns and restaurants provide the primary link with the past. These inns and restaurants also provide the visiting foreigner with the same opportunity to experience *The Japanese Way*.

Few Westerners can spend even a day in the traditional setting of Japan without being powerfully affected by the spell of its unique charm. After a while, the lure of the traditional Japanese lifestyle begins to exercise an attraction on many that is almost mystic.

I have tried in this book to help the reader both see and feel Japan in four dimensions—its physical beauty, its humanity, its spirit, and its special pleasures. To get to really know any country not your own requires the use of more than the five common senses. One must have a special intuitive sense to absorb the finer nuances of another culture.

I have always felt that I had this extrasensory perception in regard to Japan (in fact, deep in my mind I have the nagging notion that I once *was* Japanese). So my aim here has also been to share with you at least some of the enjoyment this special affinity gives me—and hopefully, to influence you to go to Japan to see and feel for yourself.

CHAPTER I

Kami-Sama No Kuni
Land of the Gods

The Age of the Gods

According to early chronicles and myths, the Japanese islands were created by a god and a goddess, *Izanagi* (ee-zah-nah-ghee) and *Izanami* (ee-zah-nah-me), who so admired their own handiwork that they descended from heaven to live on the islands. The godly couple then gave birth to the gods of the sun and the moon, of storms and of fire, and finally to lesser *kami* (kah-me) gods who became the ancestors of the Japanese.

This ancient legend establishes very early in their history that the Japanese were overwhelmingly impressed with the stunning natural beauty of their land, and that they also regarded themselves as extraordinary people. They were right in both instances.

The early Japanese believed that all natural objects and phenomena were ordained with some degree of divine spirit, and that it was necessary to live in harmony with nature in order to avoid upsetting the natural balance. Their reverence for nature and beauty was to permeate the Japanese way of life from top to bottom, and to color the

1

entire cultural fabric down to the present time.

Historically speaking, Japan's "Age of the Gods" ended in B.C. 660 when the "grandson" of the Sun Goddess became the master of southern and central Japan by force of arms, and set himself up as *Tenno* (tane-no), which is usually translated as "Emperor," but means the "Royal Son of Heaven."

The common people in the new kingdom (those who could not trace their ancestry directly to *kami*) were known as *ryomin* (rio-mean) or "good people." And at that time, the main body of Japanese called their country *Yamato* (yah-mah-toe) or "Great Peace." This later became *Nihon* (nee-hone) or *Nippon* (neep-pone), which means "Source of the Sun" (as seen from China). It is the Chinese form of *Nippon*, namely *Jih-pen*, that the modern word "Japan" comes from.

The Land the Gods Created

The most outstanding physical feature of "the lands the gods created" is its great mountain chains, its towering volcanic peaks, and the relatively broad plains on the islands of Honshu (hone-shuu) and Hokkaido (hoke-kie-doe). Much to the surprise of most visitors, four-fifths of Japan (which is larger than Italy and only slightly smaller than France) is made up of mountains of natural and volcanic origin, with an immense range running through each of the major islands.

To get a good idea of the topography of the islands, imagine each one of them with a high backbone of mountains in the center and ranges of smaller mountains radiating outward toward the coasts. Rivers originating in the mountains flow down the opposite sides, forming numerous narrow valleys and small coastal plains that are separated from each other by rugged ridges and headlands.

On the main island of Honshu, the greatest of these natural mountain ranges, characterized by sheer cliffs and peaks up to nine thousand feet in height, are known as the Northern, Central, and Southern Alps—because of their similarity to the Alps of Switzerland. While these and other natural mountains of Japan are among the world's grandest beauty spots, it is the volcanic mountains that provide the special flavor of the country's topography.

Altogether, there are seven large volcanic systems (with nearly two hundred volcanoes) running through the islands. The best known of these, of course, is the Mt. Fuji system, which begins in Niigata (nee-gah-tah) Prefecture northwest of Tokyo, includes the *Hakone* (hah-koe-nay) Mountains, the mountains of the *Izu* (ee-zoo) Peninsula south of Tokyo, the Seven Isles of Izu, Mt. Mihara on Oshima Island in Tokyo Bay, and goes all the way to Guam in the Pacific Ocean.

The great plains of Japan are the *Kanto* (kahn-toe) which surrounds Tokyo and Yokohama; the *Niigata* (nee-gah-tah) in Niigata Prefecture; the *Nobi* (no-bee) around Nagoya and Gifu City; the *Sendai* (sen-die) in northeastern Honshu; and the *Ishikari* (ee-she-kah-ree) in Hokkaido. The important cities of Kyoto, Yamagata, and Kofu are in great basins.

One of Japan's most impressive and inspiring sights is any one of a dozen of the famous views of Mt. Fuji, its tallest mountain, which at 12,365 feet stands over the islands like a national monument symbolizing the spirit and purpose that unite the country.

The Fabulous Coasts, Rivers, and Lakes

The divine creators of Japan also outdid themselves when they fashioned the coastlines. Altogether Japan has 16,120 miles of seacoast that alternates between white-sand beaches bordered by groves of gnarled green pines, precipitous cliffs also clad in pines, lagoon-like bays dotted with emerald islets, secluded coves and inlets bounded by jagged walls of stone, along with caves, caverns, natural "bridges" and "gates" sculpted from fantastic rock formations. There are unsurpassed seascapes which include numerous offshore islands anchored in blue water and ringed with surf breaking white on black rocks.

Without exaggeration, seemingly unending stretches of Japan's coastline are so extraordinarily beautiful that many who are more finely attuned find themselves intoxicated by the sight.

Another source of aesthetic intoxication in Japan are the bountiful rivers and streams (excluding the larger ones where they pass through great industrial cities—the *Yodo* (yoe-doe) in Osaka and the *Sumida* (sue-me-dah) in Tokyo). Being exceedingly mountainous with high rain and snow falls, Japan has hundreds of rivers and streams, but they are mostly short and swift. The longest river is the *Shinano* (she-nah-no), which begins at the foot of *Mt. Kobushi* (koe-buu-she) north of Tokyo, and enters the Sea of Japan at Niigata City, 229 miles away. The *Tone* (toe-nay), which begins in the *Tango* (tahn-go) Mountains and flows into the sea at Choshi adjoining Tokyo, is responsible for the largest river basin in Japan and is only two hundred miles long.

Because of the tree-covered mountain terrain, particularly in the areas that are volcanic in origin, the majority of Japan's streams and rivers pass through regions of unbounded beauty. Many are marked by rapids that provide some of the most exciting riverboating in the world. Some of the rivers that have mountain lakes as their sources drop in cascades, like canal locks in reverse, down to the sea. Literally hundreds of these streams, their waters sparkling clear and cool even in midsummer, rush through deep, heavily wooded gorges that have a rare beauty which seems unique to Japan.

Practically all of Japan's famous resort spas are located on, or within a short distance from, a river or stream, on a site especially picked for its exceptional beauty. A number that I have been to are built over trout-filled streams, allowing guests to fish from their lanais; streams, filled with huge multicolored carp, take circuitous courses through enclosed garden patios.

Japan is also rich in lakes, many formed by water collecting in volcanic calderas and by the damming of rivers by ancient lava flows. The largest of the lakes is *Biwa* (bee-wah)—260 square miles—near Kyoto. The deepest lake (1,275 feet) is *Tazawa* (tah-zah-wah) in northern Honshu.

Among the most famous of Japan's lakes are the five looped around the waist of Mt. Fuji. The queen of these is *Ashi* (ah-she), popularly known as Lake Hakone because it is high in the Hakone Mountains. Lying deep in a giant tree-lined crater, with Mt. Fuji looming majestically over it like a stairway to the heavens, Lake Hakone is frequently ringed with snow in the winter and often mist-shrouded in all seasons. Just as often it leaves its viewers speechless with admiration of its beauty.

The Kaleidoscope of Color

A great part of the natural beauty of Japan is provided by its colors, which are tuned to the seasons. The primary color of Japan is some nuance of green—leaf green, pine-needle green, grass green, or grain green, the latter waxing and waning from spring to fall. The other color that is permanently on display is the brilliant blue of the coastal waters, attached to the beaches, headlands, and sea-cliffs by ribbons of frothy white.

The next most conspicuous color is that of the snow that blankets great expanses of Hokkaido and Honshu for months during the winter, turning the tree-covered mountains and open tablelands into shimmering seas of crystal white. Then there are the hues of fall, which stir the Japanese soul with their message of the fate of all living things.

First to herald the approach of fall are the quilt-patch paddy fields of rice which ripen to a dusky yellow. Then beginning in Hokkaido and moving south, as sap withdraws from trees to begin the winter-long hibernation, large segments of Japan's mantle of green leaves change color like so many chameleons, and almost before your eyes forests of fir, spruce, beech, maple, and other species blush brilliant shades of red, gold, and brown. For several weeks thereafter, Japan is a kaleidoscope of colors, as the plumage of autumn competes for a while with the remaining coat of evergreens.

Another source of color that adds so much to the distinctive Japanese countryside are roofing tiles. Especially as you travel by train from Tokyo toward Kyoto and other southwestern destinations, you pass above clusters of homes, in fields and in innumerable glens and glades, that are topped with eye-catching patterns of ceramic tile cast in deep blue, purple, aquamarine, or pastel tints that delight the eye.

Altogether, the distinctive topography and the exceptional natural beauty of the islands of Japan provide a key ingredient in the unique culture that has developed on them.

CHAPTER II

Kisetsu No Bunka
The Seasonal Culture

The Siberian Winds

Another important key to understanding and appreciating Japan is knowing the role that climate has played in shaping the attitudes and character of the people, and how it traditionally related to their everyday life.

From the northern tip of Hokkaido (from which the Russian-held Siberian island of Sakhalin is visible) to Kagoshima on the southern edge of Kyushu, Japan stretches some 1,860 miles in a north to southwesterly direction. Hokkaido is at approximately the same latitude as the state of Maine in the U.S., and has similar weather—cool summers and long, cold winters with an abundance of snow.

The main island of Honshu parallels the eastern seaboard of the U.S. from about New York down to South Carolina, but the island has two distinct types of weather. The great ridge of mountains that run more or less north-south down the center of the island serves as a barrier blocking the cold, moisture-laden winter winds that sweep across the narrow Sea of Japan from Siberia, causing them to lose their water content in the form of snow on the west

7

side of this barrier and atop the mountains themselves. This area is Japan's fabled *Yuki Guni* (yuu-kee guu-nee) or "Snow Country," where deep snows are the main fact of life from late November to April each year.

The South Pacific Current

In addition to the protection offered by the great mountain barrier, the side of Japan facing the Pacific Ocean has another benefactor—the famous *Kuroshio* (kuu-roe-she-oh), or "Black Current," which streams up from the South Pacific, bathing the eastern seaboard in warming waters. The *Miura* (mee-uu-rah) and *Izu* (ee-zoo) peninsulas, which protrude out into this warm current just south of Tokyo, enjoy a mostly mild winter climate that has made them famous for centuries.

Official pronouncements on the subject of Japan's weather—which are often faithfully repeated in travel literature—state that Japan has a "mild" climate. This is true only in a relative sense, and then only in certain southern districts.

Winters on the Pacific side of the islands from Kagoshima at the southern tip of Kyushu to about one hundred miles north of Tokyo are distinguished by dry, sunny days alternating with short rainy, windy periods. As one moves inland and northward, light snows at lower altitudes and heavier snows in the mountains are characteristic. Temperatures even in the southern regions and along the coast may be mild one day and very cold the next.

Spring throughout the islands is changeable. Sunny clear days alternate with light to heavy rains that may continue for days. There is considerable rainfall from around the end of May to early July. Summer brings hot, humid days at lower altitudes throughout the southern islands and on Honshu as far north as the jumping-off point for Hokkaido. Typhoons, in the form of heavy rains and winds, regularly sweep the islands from late summer to early November, with September being "Typhoon Month."

In the southern and central portions of the islands, autumn brings many clear, cool days, and is generally the most comfortable time of the year. Northern Honshu and Hokkaido have brief, crisp autumns, with snow beginning in the mountains as early as October.

The four seasons in Japan are thus very pronounced, and the Japanese have always been acutely aware of this. Popular writer Shunkichi Akimoto, in his delightful book, *Exploring the Japanese Ways of Life,* says theirs is a "seasonal culture" and that their "season mindedness" is one of the primary characteristics of the Japanese. To even vaguely appreciate the traditional manifestations of Japanese thought and behavior, one must be familiar with this seasonal culture.

The Golden Tranquility of Fall

Apparently long before the Japanese began recording their history, they had already developed as a national characteristic a delicate sense of the seasons that colored every phase and facet of their lives. Until the end of the last century there was hardly any thought or action that was not somehow hinged to one of the seasons. As Akimoto-san says, there was literally a proper season for almost everything.

Because of their vivid awareness of the fragility and impermanence of life, and probably because it also meant relief from the heat and humidity of summer, the Japanese have always been especially attracted to autumn. The early morning and evening chill of the air, the leaves beginning to change color, the shortening of the shadows at sunset, and perhaps (in the words of Shunkichi Akimoto) "a flight of wild geese cruising across the skies forming a long two-line wedge headed by a queen or kingly leader" were tinged with an exquisite sadness that struck an exceptionally responsive chord in the soul of the Japanese.

Probably the best-known autumn custom, which began in Japan in prehistoric times and has continued down to the present-day, is that of celebrating the beauty of the full fall moon—popularly known as "Moon-Viewing." The moon-viewing ceremony traditionally included making special offerings to household shrines, eating special foods, and exchanging delicacies with friends and neighbors—practices that have waned considerably in recent decades, but are still followed by a devoted few.

The highlight of moon-viewing is a gathering of a few select friends at some spot where the view of the moon is extraordinarily impressive, to eat and drink, and while gazing at the moon, to compose poetry honoring its special beauty.

One can get a good idea of the popularity and importance of this custom from the fact that hundreds of places around the country have been noted as moon-viewing spots for centuries.

There are two particularly expressive Japanese words that are intimately associated with fall: *sabishii* (sah-bee-shee) and *shinmiri* (sheen-me-ree). The first of these words means "loneliness" plus a type of "emptiness" which is used to describe the feeling that often assails the more sensitive Japanese with the coming of the first signs of fall. The Japanese do not try to avoid or relieve this feeling of loneliness or emptiness. They cater to it. Moon-viewing, insect-hearing (listening to the singing of insects), and autumnal pilgrimages to remote mountain shrines—popular fall pastimes—are fraught with the sense of studied melancholy which serves to repair the life-worn spirits of the Japanese.

Shinmiri is also a commonly used colloquial word and refers to a type of atmosphere that is charged with intimate tranquility and sad contentment which is characteristic of Japan's traditional lifestyle. As expressed in my book, *Japanese Secrets of Graceful Living:* "The idea of passing time alone, austerely, while letting one's mind dwell on nostalgic events of the past, or giving up the hectic life of the city for a quiet rustic type of existence in some isolated countryside is not unique to Japan, but no other people crave it like the Japanese. As a result of this craving, the Japanese attempt to create the atmosphere in their surroundings, their music, and their literature.

"Rain is often one of the most important ingredients of a *shinmiri* atmosphere. An afternoon spent sitting quietly in a Japanese-style room that looks out over a garden, field, or valley that is being pelted by a late fall rain is certain to be flooded with a strong feeling of *shinmiri*."

The Mystique of Winter

Until about 1950 the Japanese seemed to have regarded their climate as semitropical if not tropical, and often appeared to ignore the low temperatures of winter. Homes were not built to retain heat and no effort was made to heat them. All during winter in Tokyo and other cities of central and southern Japan (except during blowing rainstorms) the custom was (and still is in many homes) to open all windows and outside sliding doors the first thing in the morning and leave them open for several hours.

On the coldest days, porcelain *hibachi* (he-bah-chee) braziers filled with smoldering charcoal were used to warm the hands. In more affluent homes, *hibachi* were also placed in covered pits in the floor called *kotatsu* (koe-taht-sue) into which one extended his legs and arms for warmth. Everyone wore several layers of clothing to keep the body warm.

Rather than trying to ward off winter with its rigors, the Japanese found ways to enjoy its special aspects. The two most noted winter customs, practiced as national observances, were *yuki-mi* (yuu-kee-me), or snow-viewing, and plum blossom-viewing. Among the upper classes, the first snow of the year was marked by groups getting together at special places to admire its beauty and compose *haiku* (hie-kuu) poetry commemorating the transcendental beauty of the fragile crystals.

One of the most attractive and common types of stone lanterns found in the gardens of private homes and inns was designed to be lighted during or following snowfalls so that occupants could enjoy the sight even at night. Snow thus became a means for the Japanese to practice aesthetic appreciation.

Plum blossom-viewing, in March when the trees are in full bloom, was a popular custom as far back as 800 A.D., and although considerably diminished, remains today an important exercise in aestheticism for many Japanese. The blossoms, appearing naked and fragile amidst the snow and wind of late winter, are said by Shunkichi Akimoto to symbolize for the Japanese the virtues of chastity, courage, and austerity under adverse conditions.

Another winter scene that the Japanese have traditionally admired, and around which they developed specific customs, was the combining of snow with sprigs of pine, bamboo, and plum in numerous decorative functions.

Today, the main winter celebration is *Oshogatsu* (oh-show-got-sue), New Years, which is marked by visits to shrines and the homes of relatives and friends, giving gifts, eating special foods, and visiting ancestral homes. On New Year's night, hundreds of thousands of people flock to noted shrines in their area to mark the end of the old year and the beginning of the new.

At some of the great shrines around the country, hundreds of young men, usually dressed only in loincloths despite the generally frigid temperatures, participate in bell-ringing ceremonies that are televised nationally and provide one of the most exciting spectacles to be seen in Japan. Some of these temple bells are immense in size, with their clappers consisting of giant logs suspended on ropes from the ceiling. There is nothing quite like the far-carrying sound of one of these great bells, and to me there is no more poignant reminder of how intimately Japan's present is linked with its past.

The Cherry Blossom Spring

For nearly a thousand years the coming of spring in Japan has been marked by parties held beneath canopies of cherry trees. In earlier centuries, some of the greatest social and cultural events in the country's history were cherry blossom parties held at famous viewing places. References to cherry blossoms in the novels and poetry of Japan are legend.

The fragile pink petals of the cherry tree long ago came to symbolize for the Japanese not only the incomparable beauty of nature but also the impermanence of all things, especially the tenuous hold man has on life. Formal occasions to celebrate the beauty and characteristics of the blossoms first developed among the privileged classes in the eleventh century, and by the 1600s had spread downward to include the common people.

Eventually cherry blossom-viewing became a genuine cult and was just as influential in its own way as the more famous "Cult of the Sword" which developed around the use of that weapon during the long supremacy of Japan's *Samurai* warrior class from 1192 A.D. until recent times. In no other country has a blossom ever played such an imposing role.

Still today, millions of Japanese each spring hold outings beneath the short-lived blossoms. Women dress in their gayest kimono. Box lunches, along with spiritous drinks, are taken or bought on the spot from mobile vendors. Except among the more serious aesthetes, these parties are not sedate, calm affairs at which the participants sit around quietly contemplating the beauty and fragility of the blossoms and tossing off equally fragile poetry. The majority of the occasions have traditionally been accompanied by unrestrained indulgence in *O'sake* (oh-sah-kay) rice wine, especially by men, who take the lead in singing popular folksongs and dancing.

This popular sensual and aesthetic celebration usually begins in Kagoshima on the southern end of Kyushu in late March and advances up the island chain with the season, ending in Hokkaido in June.

In Tokyo some of the more famous cherry blossom-viewing spots include Shinjuku Gyoen Gardens, Ueno Park, and Chidorigafuchi Park. The huge Imperial Palace grounds in the center of Tokyo are also ringed by cherry trees, providing passersby with the opportunity to enjoy the beauty of the blossoms daily for several days without going out of their way.

One of the most noted cherry blossom-viewing spots in the Kyoto area is Arashi Mountain on the outskirts of the city. Probably the most famous viewing place in the country is at Yoshino in Nara Prefecture, an hour from either Osaka or Kyoto, where an entire valley and mountainside are covered with a profusion of cherry trees. The trees, numbering around 100,000 and appearing in four groves, were first planted in the latter part of the seventh century by a priest named En-no-Ozunu.

The Season to Be *Assari*

The style of life that the Japanese developed for summer is closely associated with the word *assari* (ahs-sah-ree), which means "simple, frank, brief," and "light-hearted and relaxed." Among the summer cooling diversions—*suzumi* (sue-zoo-me)—were swimming, fishing, mountain-hiking, strolling along rivers and mountain streams, eating light meals, thinking light thoughts, attending open-air theatrical performances and neighborhood festivals, relating ghost stories to send chills up each other's backs, and attending ghost plays at theaters.

The summer *assari* customs that were especially popular in the evenings, after the day's work was done, are described by the word *yusuzumi* (yuu-sue-zoo-me), which means something like "enjoying the cool of the evening." To practice *yusuzumi* it was first of all necessary for one to wipe his mind clean of all events of the day just ending. The next step was to take a hot bath followed by a drenching in cool water, then don a clean *yukata* (yu-kah-tah) robe and take up a small fan that had been delicately scented with the aroma of pine.

Once a person had cleansed both body and mind, he was ready for the next step—idle contemplation. While contemplating, he might sit and listen to the sounds peculiar to a summer evening—birds in the trees, insects in the garden grass, children playing in the distance, the tinkling of a windbell, or the gurgle of running water. One could stroll in his garden or along the banks of a nearby stream.

The idea was to relax completely and refresh one's self by forgetting all worldly cares so that the discomfort of the summer heat would disappear into the lengthening shadows.

Certainly not all Japanese follow these traditional summer practices of *yusuzumi* today. In urban areas, most have air-conditioning in their homes or apartments. But there are those who do, especially in rural areas and suburbs of the cities, and the attitude remains strongly entrenched.

One of the most popular and enduring of the *yusuzumi* practices of Japan is watching and participating in the colorful *Bon Odori* (bone oh-doe-ree) or Bon Dance, which is a type of community folk-dancing that originated centuries ago in relation to ancestor worship. Although its religious connotations have been forgotten, it is still performed throughout Japan during mid-July in urban areas and in mid-August in the countryside.

A temporary bandstand, usually elevated on high poles, is erected in the neighborhood temple grounds. The area is festooned with colorful paper lanterns and bunting. Music is provided by a group dressed in traditional costumes—or in some cases today, by a tape deck. Residents of the neighborhood, mostly dressed in the cool, comfortable *yukata*, gather at the grounds at about dusk, and for the next two or three hours watch, stroll about, and dance to the nostalgic, haunting melodies of Old Japan.

In many areas near water, the annual Obon Festival includes *Toro Nagashi* (toe-roe nah-gah-she), or "the Floating of the Lanterns," during which small candlelit lanterns on tiny rafts are set loose on the water.

CHAPTER III

Ninhonjin No Kao
Faces of the Japanese

The People Make the Difference

During the many years that I have been connected with Japan and intimately concerned with the country as a travel area, it has been my experience that an overwhelming majority of the well-traveled people who go there for pleasure later say it is by far the best; that no other country compares. When questioned in detail about why they feel this way, most of the travelers finally end up saying, "Because the people are so wonderful."

My own opinion is that the unique appeal of Japan is a combination of the character and customs of the people, the distinctive food, the traditional dress, the Japanese inn, the aesthetic charm of the arts and crafts, and so on. But I have also personally known dozens of Westerners who did not appreciate any of these latter things and yet stayed on in Japan for years, unwilling to leave despite their many dislikes.

While it would be easy to dismiss this particular group as being attracted to Japan only because of the cultural emphasis on sex and the sexual permissiveness they are able to participate in, this would not be the whole truth and would be unfair to my friends and acquaintances as well as to the Japanese. For there is actually a great deal more than sexual pleasure involved in the relationships these people have with Japan, and one way or another it can all be traced to the traditional character, personality, and manners of the people.

The Japanese are extraordinarily conscious of their racial differences and of their distinctive culture, and they habitually distinguish between what is "native" and what has been imported from the West. These same differences are also very conspicuous to the Western visitor, who often is even more inclined to discriminate between what he perceives to be Japanese and non-Japanese. One result of this situation is that both the faults and the good points of the Japanese and "things Japanese" are constantly being emphasized. Of course, it is the "good points" that exercise an almost hypnotic attraction on the visitor from abroad.

Racial Heritage of the Japanese

It is generally agreed that the Japanese are a mixture of four racial groups: two distinctively Mongoloid groups from the mainland of Asia; a Malay-Negrito stock from Southeast Asia who first settled in Kyushu; and the *Ainu* (aye-new), a Caucasoid race who were apparently the original inhabitants of the islands (possibly from the age when the islands were still attached to the Asian continent).

Contrary to a common stereotyped image, the Japanese do not all look alike, although there are fewer extremes in their general appearance and features than are seen in the U.S. and most European countries.

The Japanese generally have black or deep auburn colored hair, slender builds, and the characteristic Oriental eye to varying degrees. Beyond this there are conspicuous differences in height, complexion, individual facial features, and figures. For the average Westerner it requires only a few hours, or days at most, to switch from identifying individuals by their body builds, hair color, and voice to looking more closely at the finer features of their faces.

For a racial and ethnic group that has been called physically unattractive by some of its own artists and writers who have lived and traveled abroad (the most celebrated case being a former ambassador who wrote a book in which he said his fellow countrymen reminded him of monkeys), Japan has traditionally produced some of the world's more beautiful women—by anyone's standards. The Kyoto and Tohoku areas are especially noted for the extraordinary beauty of their women.

At any rate, the faces and figures of the Japanese have been undergoing remarkable changes since the 1950s, and old descriptions are no longer valid. Younger generations are taller and heavier than their parents. The figures of the girls are becoming more voluptuous and those of the boys more muscular.

The Shinto Theme in Japanese Character

Shintoism, the native religion, played a vital role in shaping the basic character of the Japanese, and subsequently the unique Japanese civilization. The myth of the divine origin of Japan and the Japanese, which stands at the center of Shintoism, has already been mentioned. Other essential facets of Shintoism include a deep reverence for all aspects of nature from both a spiritual and an aesthetic viewpoint, along with a special concern for the fertility of living things. Fertility festivals were common until recent times, and still may be seen in both urban and rural areas around the country. Phallic symbols, especially the erect male organ, were common throughout the islands at intersections of roads and other well-traveled places.

Shintoism stresses ritual purity, and is a cheerful, optimistic, happy religion. Its festivals are more like carnivals than religious observances. Food stalls, booths selling souvenirs and novelty items, singing, dancing, and drinking are characteristic of Shinto festivals.

In Shintoism, mountains are regarded as sacred places because, according to ancient myths, they are where souls go after death. This belief led to the building of shrines on mountain tops and in high places in general, from hills to even low mounds rising abruptly out of level plains.

The ranking Shinto shrine in Japan is the *Grand Shrine of Ise* (ee-say), where the spirits of dead emperors are enshrined. The shrine is in such a beautiful location that Japan author Donald Keene once noted that its beauty alone was enough to ensure faith in the Shinto gods. The buildings of the Ise Shrine are rebuilt every twenty years. They were rebuilt for the sixtieth time in 1973.

Along with its emphasis on fertility, Shintoism also incorporates a deep respect for the soul of man, a view of mankind as brothers responsible for each other's welfare and happiness, and a vision of complete tranquility and peace.

All of the well over 100,000 Shinto shrines in Japan are marked by the presence of a *torii* (toe-ree), the familiar "gate" consisting of two upright columns and one or two pieces across the top, depending on the style. Shinto priests wear robes of white or pastel colors (Buddhist priests wear black). Worshipers do not enter the shrine when paying their respects. They simply bow before the shrine and clap their hands to attract the attention of the enshrined spirit or god before making a silent prayer, then make an offering of money to the shrine coffers.

The Buddhist Theme

Buddhism was introduced into Japan from China in the sixth century A.D., and over the next several hundred years most Japanese became Buddhists as well as Shintoist. Buddhism had a profound influence on the culture and civilization of Japan, serving as the medium for the introduction of new ideas regarding handicrafts, architecture, art, wearing apparel, festivals, burial customs, and perhaps most important of all, a system of writing, which led to the beginning of written literature. Buddhism also introduced, particularly in the twelfth and thirteenth centuries, new ways of looking at the questions of life and death.

One of these new approaches to living was bound up in the Zen sect of Buddhism, which in simple terms aims at bringing the body, mind, and spirit into perfect harmony with each other and the world at large. Zen teaches that this goal is to be achieved by first gaining control of the mind, conditioning it to perceive things as they really are, then making one's life an extension of this knowledge.

Zen thereafter became the leavening in the distinctive character of the Japanese civilization, providing them with another philosophy, another ethical foundation, a final arbiter in matters of taste, and a means of gaining extraordinary mastery in such skills as calligraphy, painting, gardening, utensil-making, and even swordfighting.

Under the influence of Zen, the Japanese strove to perfect a "cult" of spiritual and intellectual tranquility and to recognize the true essence of things by means of continuous self-discipline and control over their emotions and desires. They made many of the ordinary actions of life into exercises in mental control and composure, and developed a series of special exercises aimed at making perfect tranquility a permanent state of mind.

The Confucian Theme

Confucianism, a semireligious ethic system also introduced into Japan from China (some authorities say in 285 A.D.), was responsible for the establishment in Japan of what has been referred to as "the cult of the family," which taught that filial piety was the highest virtue, and resulted in a form of ancestor worship.

This filial piety was owed to parents as well as to the sovereign, who was the symbolic father of all. The state was seen as an extended version of the family. Behavior toward superiors, equals, and inferiors was prescribed in a strict code of manners.

Confucianism taught that man was innately good (the opposite of Christianity?), and that he needed only instruction and example to behave properly and avoid evil—not threats and punishment, which are the hallmarks of the Christian religion. Confucianism was thus more compatible with the Japanese than Buddhism, and gradually pushed the latter into the background. Confucianism is credited with giving impetus to a renaissance of learning and refinement of the Japanese culture that took place during the 265-year reign of the Tokugawa feudal government (1603–1868).

While most Japanese today do not claim any particular religious affiliation, Japanese culture as a whole is a mixture of Shintoism, Buddhism, and Confucianism. All of Japan's hundreds of festivals and ceremonial functions that are so much a part of the life of every Japanese are derived from one or another of these three streams of thought. At the same time, there are several Buddhist-oriented sects that have active memberships numbering in the millions.

The Aesthetic Theme

For some unknown reason, the Japanese were very early endowed with an extraordinary regard for natural beauty. Other cultures have developed within scenic surroundings but none except the Japanese has ever made the appreciation of beauty into a national pastime and an art in itself. As noted in my *Japanese Secrets of Graceful Living*: "From earliest times the Japanese engaged in regular exercises for developing their aesthetic sense and for appreciating beauty—a phenomenon so unusual in the world that this alone would have been enough to make them unique."

It was apparently their highly developed regard for nature and their devotion to natural beauty that led the Japanese to fashion a culture in which a natural type of functional beauty became characteristic of their tools, utensils, handicrafts, decorative items, and buildings. Ordinary bowls and trays produced over two thousand years ago for everyday kitchen or household use had what we now refer to as classical beauty. This output of highly artistic utilitarian products is said to have been "prodigious" by the eighth century.

Whatever its source, this preoccupation with beauty, refined by Zen concepts to the essence of naturalness and simplicity, is one of the most powerful and conspicuous themes of life in Japan. The adoration of beauty as seen in nature reached its climax in the various blossom-viewing practices and especially in the tea ceremony, where the practice of aesthetics is combined with a physical and mental discipline based on a total philosophy of life.

The Tea Ceremony

In fact, Japan's extraordinary dedication to aesthetics became epitomized in the now famous—but often misunderstood—*Cha-no Yu* or "tea ceremony." In their cultural shortsightedness, many of the first Westerners to visit Japan discounted and criticized the tea ceremony because they didn't like the taste of the tea that was served.

The tea ceremony, already a popular "cult" in the sixteenth century, has as its primary purpose the teaching of gracefulness and inner harmony, the understanding and appreciation of true beauty, and finally, recognition and appreciation of man's relation with nature.

A typical tea ceremony includes a tea master or student of the art and a few guests. The host makes all of the preparations in advance, in a small room or detached house designed and built for the purpose. Customarily the guests enter the room in the order of their reputation for cultural refinement, their age, or their relationship with the host.

There is no talking. The aim is to achieve complete physical and mental relaxation. When the tea is ready, the host serves the guests in a ceremonial manner dating back to the time of the great tea master Sen-no Rikyu (1521–1591). Then the ranking guest asks permission to examine the tea implements. These are placed in front of the guests, who attempt to merge their consciousness with the simple naturalness and beauty of the implements.

The host then bows his guests out, prepares a cup of tea for himself, and, as described in *Japanese Secrets of Graceful*

Living, "drinks it in solitude, savoring the thick, astringent brew, the quiet lonely mood, and the setting until the last measure of aesthetic joy is his."

There are a number of *Cha-no Yu* "schools" in Japan today, all doing a flourishing business. Two of the best known are *Omote Senke* (oh-moe-tay sain-kay) and *Ura Senke* (uu-rah sain-kay), originally founded in Kyoto by the same tea master, and then split into separate schools by the master's descendants—at first in the same building (*omote* means "front" and *ura* means "back"), where they were lodged for a long time.

The Japanese Concept of Beauty

The distinctive Japanese concept of beauty came to be described by the term *shibui* (she-booey), which means something like "astringent" and "restrained," and refers to a stark simplicity and naturalness that reveals the essence of a thing.

To the Japanese, beauty and naturalness are practically synonymous. Anything that is unnatural cannot be beautiful, but at the same time, beauty may be enhanced by accenting certain natural qualities.

The Japanese are especially sensitive to signs of age, such as the bleached color of driftwood, moss on a rock or tree, the twisted body of an ancient pine tree, or the parched, wrinkled face of an old person.

The Japanese express the appearance and feeling of age by the word *sabi* (sah-bee) which literally means "rust." To them, objects that are "rusty" with age are particularly beautiful. Japanese craftsmen deliberately build this quality into many of their wares.

Another quality of beauty as seen by the Japanese is expressed by the term *wabi* (wah-bee), which is an abbreviation of *wabishi* (wah-bee-she) and means "wretched, desolate," or "lonely." A further quality that the Japanese demand in beauty is one that lies below the surface in a very delicate harmony that is visible only to the person whose aesthetic abilities are highly trained. This quality is often referred to as *yugen* (yuu-gain), which means "mystery" or "subtlety."

Finally, there is another ancient Japanese word that is intimately linked with their view of beauty. This is *myo* (me-yoe), which might be described as the "soul" of an object, and which usually cannot be perceived by anyone with a strong ego.

With the Japanese, the practice of aesthetics was never a sometime or part-time thing. For centuries it permeated every aspect of their lives—from the arrangement of food on a serving tray or table to the decorations on their sliding wall panels.

The *tokonoma* (toe-koe-no-mah) is another thing unique to Japan. It began as an alcove-shrine in the main room of homes. By the fifteenth century it had become a special area reserved for the display of different art objects—one at a time and changed with the occasion or season. Japan thus became the only country in the world in which every home, no matter how modest or mean, had a place permanently set aside for the display of beauty.

The appreciation of beauty and the rules by which true beauty is judged are no longer overriding themes in the lives of the average Japanese, but they are still very much in evidence. Aestheticism continues unabated in the side of Japanese life that is traditional, and its influence makes itself felt in many areas of Japanese life that are Western. Tokyo's finest hotels, for example, owe much of their distinctive attraction to a subtle blending of Western-style accommodations and traditional Japanese concepts of interior decoration.

On a very practical level, the aesthetic traditions and conditioning of the Japanese make them very sensitive to the appearance and quality of all the modern-day products they make and buy—which is one of the reasons products made in the West with less attention to design and quality do not sell better in Japan.

"Living Flowers"

Probably the best known of the techniques the Japanese developed to train and practice their aesthetic abilities is the so-called "flower arranging," or *Ike Bana*, which literally means "Living Flowers." Ike Bana is said to date from a suggestion made by Emperor Saga in the ninth century, and still today no Japanese girl is considered educated until she has gained some skill in this gentle art.

The techniqe of *Ike Bana* consists of arranging flowers in such a way that they seem to be alive and growing. In doing so, the person is required to practice patience, gracefulness, correct manners, self-control, and peace of mind. Once arranged, the *Ike Bana* are displayed for a few days in the tokonoma, where all can appreciate them and reflect on their silent message of beauty and serenity.

The Artistic Impulse

The people of traditional Japan did not try to live apart from nature or to change it. Their aim was to live with it in harmony. The architect, on whatever level, designed his buildings to merge in with the surroundings. The craftsman accented the natural characteristics of his materials. The artist tried to capture the essence of nature by emphasizing its principal outlines and letting the viewer fill in the details from his own store of experience and imagery. The poet attempted to distill the essence of a fragment of existence by presenting a single provocative image of a natural phenomenon.

Until recent decades the Japanese were religiously trained in a number of artistic skills from childhood—not in a conscious effort to develop the skills for the sake of refinement, but because it was the natural way of life. One of the most important of these skills was learning how to write their own language—first correctly, and then with artistic style.

Before the appearance of a system of writing in Japan, there was an extensive oral literature. The people at large were great storytellers and versifiers. Then a remarkable event took place. The Japanese literally adopted the pictorial writing system of the Chinese, even though their spoken languages were completely dissimilar. Learning the complicated Chinese characters required years of meticulous study and practice by each person, and resulted in making the literate person, of necessity, an artist of considerable skill.

Afterwards, the Japanese developed their own simplified system for writing their language *(hiragana)*, which was gradually combined with the much more elaborate Chinese ideograms. But for one long period in Japan's history, education, social accomplishments, even a person's morality, were judged by how well—how beautifully—he or she could write the imported Chinese characters.

As more and more common people learned how to read and write, their penchant for oral versifying was transferred to poetry writing, which developed into a national pastime. The young and old, the well-to-do and the poor, the learned and the barely literate, composed, almost compulsively it seems, to satisfy their own poetic passions as well as to share their emotions with others.

Being able to dash off a clever and evocative poem became equated with the highest cultural achievements, just as the ability with the writing brush had in earlier times. The stern *samurai* warriors were as proud, if not prouder, of their poetry-writing skills as they were of their astounding swordsmanship. Cut down on the battlefield, a warrior would often use his last few seconds of life to compose and toss a wise couplet at his enemies.

Poetry-writing schools flourished by the hundreds in Japan until the modern era began, and men like Basho, Buson, Issa, Shiki, and Tansetsu won lasting fame. Poetry-writing contests were held and attended with all the enthusiasm that accompanies one of our greatest sporting events. Finally, an annual nationwide "poetry tournament" was inaugurated, and the tournament—open to everyone—continues today. Participants number in the dozens of thousands and include members of the imperial family down to grade-school students in remote mountain communities.

Singing was traditionally a part of the everyday life of the Japanese. Still today, many Japanese children can carry a tune and sing before they can talk well (because their mothers, grandmothers, and other family members are always singing to them). Most of them know dozens of songs by heart by the time they reach their teens, and are old hands at singing alone and in groups at parties and other festive occasions.

Singing was also closely associated with work in Japan. There were special songs, handed down for generations, for virtually every type of traditional job, and often differing with the region of the country. Sometimes, as in the case of farmers, fishermen, and carpenters, who are regularly called upon to do very hard work, these songs were ritualistic in nature and served to provide them with a rhythmic beat to follow in their movements. In other cases, the songs—and often singsong cries—were used by trades-men to identify themselves and their wares, a custom that continues today.

Get a group of Japanese together for any casual or re-creational purpose and they almost invariably end up sing-ing.

From earliest times, dancing was also an integral part of Japanese life. Children received informal instruction in how to dance at a very early age. By the time they were three or four years old, they naturally joined in the dancing at the frequent festivals. These folk-dances required the attainment of considerable grace, and until recent decades no Japanese—unless they were physically handicapped—could reach adulthood without being able to perform well enough in public to avoid embarrassment.

In addition to casual folk-dancing, classical dancing has long been a vital part of Japanese culture, and still today helps to shape the character and manners for which the Japanese are noted. Classical dancing is an integral part of several forms of Japanese theater, and is also part of the training of many young girls. The profession of dance teacher is an honored one, and there are many schools (styles) of dancing in Japan today.

Although the custom of everyone learning how to dance, by natural osmosis as well as formal study, has changed, particularly in urban areas and among boys, the vast ma-jority of the Japanese can still put on a pretty good exhibi-tion of folk-dancing when the occasion arises.

The Kindness Cult

Despite some contradictions in their character, the Japa-nese are among the kindest and most helpful of all people, especially when compared to some of the industrially advanced Western nationalities. In fact, this kindness, particularly where visiting foreigners are concerned, often goes so far it becomes embarrassing because we are not used to it and do not know how to accept it graciously.

The kindness of the Japanese is a traditional thing that is deeply embedded in their culture. In the earliest historical writings of the country there are frequent mentions of the importance of kindness, and kindness is one of the Five Principles of Confucianism making up the ethical base of Japan's traditional social system (the others were filial piety, fidelity, obedience, and loyalty to superiors).

It sometimes happens that the helpful concern of the Japanese is misunderstood by a certain type of foreign visitor. Not being used to such behavior, they tend to be suspicious of it or derogatory toward it. Most visitors, however, respond spontaneously to this too rare type of behavior with great delight and a feeling of wonder. In my years of monitoring the reactions of travelers in Japan, the thing that most impresses them—actually overwhelms them in many cases—is this singular Japanese trait of unselfish kindness.

The typical Japanese behavior manifests itself in numerous ways in all areas of life. But it is especially characteristic of the various services that make up the travel and vacation industry. It is not an exaggeration to say that in Japan the customer is king.

The Philosophy of Hospitality

The secret of the special relationship that exists between customers and proprietors, clerks, and other staff in Japan is bound up in the word *O'kyaku* (oh-kyah-kuu), with the title *san* (sahn) attached, which means both "honored customer" and "honored guest."

In other words, in the service industries especially, the Japanese do not distinguish between guest and customer. They treat a customer with the same high respect and deference that people elsewhere usually reserve for a visiting rich uncle.

This traditional custom is one of the many things that makes traveling in Japan such a pleasurable and rewarding experience. The traveler benefits enormously not only because of this custom, but also because as an outsider who is also a guest, his status is even higher than that of a rich uncle.

The foreign visitor in Japan is regarded not just as a guest of an individual, a hotel, or a particular restaurant or shop. He or she is also quite literally viewed as a guest of Japan, which means a Very Important Person whose comfort and satisfaction is a national responsibility.

As is well known, the Japanese are a proud people and are very much concerned with "face"—which, of course, is another way of saying "reputation" or how other people regard them. This pride and concern for face is both individual and national. Each Japanese feels responsible for his or her own reputation as well as that of the country. He or she automatically goes to extraordinary lengths to protect both.

The Japanese therefore tend to feel personally obligated to help every foreign visitor enjoy the trip and get only the best impression of Japan. To a certain type of foreigner this attitude and behavior smacks of sycophancy, inferiority, and even malicious cunning, but this reaction is in error.

The kindness and hospitality of the average Japanese is spontaneous and springs from inherent goodwill and genuine concern for people. Even when this special kindness is part of the travel industry's professional service, and is calculated and emphasized, it serves exactly the same purpose and sets the Japanese apart, as one traveler after another discovers shortly after arriving in the country.

CHAPTER IV

Nihon No Tanoshimi No Koto
The Joys of Japan

The Pleasure Theme

Pleasure has traditionally been one of the primary facets of Japanese life. Shintoism embraced the concept that physical pleasures, along with the intellectual and spiritual, were an integral part of man's existence. The Japanese have taken full advantage of this recognition since ancient times.

The physical pleasures indulged in by the Japanese cover a wide range and include sex, participating in festival celebrations, visiting hot-spring spas, eating, traveling, drinking (a *lot* of drinking), playing numerous games, hiking, and more. Their traditional intellectual pleasures include the already mentioned poetry-writing, attending the theater, and such aesthetic practices as flower- and moon-viewing.

Sexual Mores

In addition to the almost hypnotic aesthetic attraction that Japan has for sensitive foreign visitors as a result of its natural and man-made beauty, there is another attraction provided by a broad, deep stream of sensuality that flows through the culture. This sensuality, which gives off a constant promise of sex, acts as a powerful stimulant, particularly to foreign men visiting the country, coloring their view of Japan and its people. Of course, this sexual stimulation is magnified by the imagination of the visitors from abroad, but the promise becomes a reality often enough that Japan more than deserves its reputation for worldly pleasures.

As noted in my *Bachelor's Japan,* the Japanese regard sex as one of the several normal human activities that is to be engaged in regularly and completely as long as it is kept in its place. Recognizing sex as an important natural function in the overall scheme of life, the Japanese have never regarded it as evil. On the contrary, it is considered unnatural and harmful for a man or woman to go without satisfying sexual relations.

At the same time, there were different sex standards for men and women. Wives were primarily for the continuation of the family, while sex for pleasure and recreation was often indulged in outside the home. A man's duties as a husband and father were traditionally separated from erotic pleasures. Marriages were arranged and love was not a consideration. For a long stage in the history of the country, a personal attachment between husbands and wives, particularly in the upper classes, was seen as a detriment to a successful marriage.

The keeping of mistresses has been a traditional feature of Japanese life, and elaborate courtesan quarters were a familiar aspect of every city until prostitution was made illegal on April 1, 1956 (with a one-year grace period). Casual sex has lost none of its popularity in present-day Japan, however, and although organized prostitution must operate behind a facade of discretion, it flourishes on both a professional and an amateur basis. Personal liaisons formed strictly for sexual pleasure, and involving people in all areas of life, are also a characteristic feature of the current scene—although the AIDS scare that finally struck Japan in 1987 put a damper on some of the institutionalized activity.

Beginning of Western-type Nightlife

There is no country in the world today where the art of entertainment and the volume and variety of nightlife surpasses that of Japan. Most people are familiar with the terms *kabuki* (kah-buu-kee) and *geisha* (gay-e-shah), but these two institutions do not begin to suggest the range of Japan's remarkable entertainment industry.

Known in colloquial Japanese as *mizu shobai* (me-zoo show-bye) or literally "water business," the entertainment trades traditionally include not only show business as such but all the enterprises engaged in selling prepared food and drink to the public. The interesting connotation is apparently that earthly pleasures may sparkle brightly for a short while, but they soon evaporate into nothing.

In ancient times, entertainment in Japan was generally divided into two categories—one associated with eating and drinking (and often sex), and the other with various forms of theater.

Prior to the early 1920s there was practically no Western-style nightlife in Japan. Then Japanese travelers returning from Europe introduced cafés directly styled after French coffee shops. Before long these cafés began serving alcoholic drinks, and soon developed into the predecessors of today's cabarets and nightclubs.

Americans introduced Western-style nightclub entertainment into Japan during the 1945–1952 military occupation, and with the passing of the licensed gay quarters in April 1957 the world of the *mizu shobai* rapidly took on its present form.

Until the late 1950s Japan's extensive entertainment trades catered almost exclusively to men. Before this, men simply did not take their wives or girlfriends out nightclubbing. Female companionship was traditionally provided by large numbers of young women employed in the "water business" as hostesses, barmaids, and waitresses.

The Geisha Today

Geisha are still a very important part of the entertainment, business, and political world in Japan today, but there have been a number of fundamental changes in the profession. Present-day geisha in the great cities operate more or less as independent businesswomen who belong to a tightly closed association. Some of them live in geisha residences. Others live in ordinary homes or apartments and commute like any other working woman.

Guests do not ordinarily go to "geisha houses" as such. They patronize a special kind of restaurant-inn called *ryotei* (rio-tay) that calls in geisha as their request. There are some restaurant-inns, however, that employ live-in geisha on a full-time basis. As in the past, the purpose of the geisha is to entertain male guests by singing, dancing, and engaging them in light, often risque, conversation.

Both Japanese politicians and older businessmen say that geisha and cabaret hostesses as well add a special "soft" or "sweet" quality to the hard facts and serious decisions they have to make, and that is why they like to have these professional women on hand when they are wheeling and dealing or have just finished a hard piece of business.

The Shimbashi geisha district is one of the best known of the more than two dozen listed districts in Tokyo, and at the last count included seventy geisha *ryotei*. Guests who call in geisha are charged by the hour, with the rate depending on the class and popularity of the individual geisha. It is said that top geisha from Shimbashi as well as the Akasaka and Yanagibashi districts earn between $150,000 and $300,000 a year. But only a small percentage of this is net income because their expenses are very high.

Geisha generally work in teams of three or four. A geisha dinner party usually lasts from three to four hours and a bill of several thousand dollars is not unusual. Geisha from less prestigious districts are not as expensive.

Licensed geisha are not prostitutes, although it is common for them to form sexual liaisons with exclusive patrons.

In addition to the registered and licensed geisha, there are large numbers of women—often referred to as "instant geisha"—who are utilized by second- and third-class *ryotei* as well as by some traditional-style restaurants that cater to foreign visitors. These women do not follow the strict etiquette code of the professional geisha.

Coffee Shop Culture

Coffee shops play an important role in Japan, both day and night. Because the Japanese do not generally meet or entertain friends or business associates at home, and because there are no private offices in most Japanese companies, coffee shops are used as a universal meeting place in Japan. Some are small nooks that seat only ten or twelve people, while others cover entire floors of large buildings.

Many coffee shops have distinctive themes that include the type of music featured, the uniforms worn by the staff, and so on. Some employ only good-looking women; others have all-male staffs. There are thousands of coffee shops in Japan's major cities, so the visitor generally has little problem finding one. The best guide is an outside sign—it may be very small and inconspicuous—that says "Coffee," since there is no telling what the front is going to look like.

After the visitor in Japan has dined, he has a wide choice of theater entertainment. Japan has been one of the world's top film producers since the 1950s, and there are over eight thousand theaters in the country. Several Japanese directors have gained international repute, and a number of Japanese films such as *The Seven Samurai* and *Rashomon* (rah-show-moan) are considered by many to be masterpieces of cinema art.

Most of Japan's entertainment districts include a number of first- and second-run theaters (the Rokku Amusement Center in Tokyo's Asakusa Ward boasts thirty theaters), and there are dozens of others scattered in main terminal areas. Some first-run theaters showing only Japanese films include English subtitles for the convenience of foreign viewers who do not understand Japanese.

Besides the movie theaters, Tokyo and Osaka have regular kabuki, noh, and bunraku or puppet performances. Kabuki plays are mostly classical dramas in which male actors perform all the roles while dressed in elaborately styled, colorful costumes.

The puppet plays of Japan are kabuki in miniature. The best puppet theaters and handlers have traditionally been in Osaka, while Tokyo is recognized as the kabuki capital. The visitor to Japan who fails to take in a kabuki performance has missed one of the world's most extraordinary theatrical experiences. Noh dramas are usually too elegant and symbolic for the general public, and most showings are attended only by private noh clubs.

Japan's two most famous revue theaters are the twin *Takarazukas* (tah-kah-rah-zoo-kahs), one in Tokyo just across the side street from the Imperial Hotel (it was the Ernie Pyle Theater during the American military occupation of Japan), and the other in Takarazuka City about an hour outside of Osaka and Kobe. The Takarazuka theaters feature hundreds of tall, beautiful girls (no males) in a variety of musical revues and dramas that attracts hundreds of thousands of people (mostly young girls) annually.

The Soaplands (Massage Bathhouses)

One of the largest and most conspicuous of Japan's pleasure industries is its so-called "Soaplands," or massage bathhouses. Most of the hundreds of soapland massage bathhouses are located in or near well-known entertainment districts. In Tokyo's Asakusa area alone there are some 150 (there are several along the expressway between Tokyo and the New Tokyo International Airport in Narita that are visible from the limousine buses serving this route). Most of the soaplands cater only to men, but there are others that welcome both men and women and some accept women only. In all of them, the general routine is similar. The patron is given a steam bath, a hot-water bath, and then a lengthy massage by a girl dressed in halter-bra and shorts—followed by some kind of sex service if the patron desires it.

All of the baths have beer and soft drinks available. Many have adjoining restaurants and offer patrons hotel-type room service facilities. Many of the baths launder the patron's underwear while he or she is being bathed and massaged.

For the uninitiated, a detailed description of the soapland routine should be useful. Most of the soaplands will accept reservations by phone. In any event, you go in and walk up to a registration counter, just as you do in a hotel. If you have a reservation and have arrived just on time, your masseuse almost immediately appears (she will be wearing a short robe over her bra and shorts) and escorts you to her private bath-massage room. If you are early or have no appointment, you may be asked to wait in a lounge area where there will be magazines and usually a television set.

The first thing you are instructed to do when you enter the tiny vestibule of the bath-room is to remove your shoes. Then the girl helps you undress and hands you a towel to wrap around your waist. She escorts you to a steam box, guides you into it, and closes the hatch-door, leaving only your head exposed. While you are steaming, she will check the hot-water bath, offer you beer or some other kind of refreshment, and wipe the sweat from your brow. When you indicate that you have had enough she will let you out of the box and direct you to enter the hot-bath.

After letting you soak for a few minutes, the girl then directs you to get out of the tub and sit down on a small stool. She then proceeds to scrub you from top to bottom, front and back. She rinses you off with numerous buckets of fresh hot water, towels you dry, then directs you to lie down on the massage bunk—usually face-down to begin with. She then massages you from your toes to your neck and fingertips for some twenty to thirty minues.

If you are going to be offered a choice of any of the special services for which the soaplands are famous, you will know shortly after she has you turn face-up. Her actions will become intimate enough that there will be no doubt when the next move is up to you. The girls can invariably communicate well enough in English to make their services and their rates known to foreign customers.

The Kimono and the Yukata

The Japanese *kimono* (kee-moe-no) and its simplified offspring the *yukata* (yuu-kah-tah) are two of Japan's most valuable tourist attractions. The predecessor of the kimono was imported from China more than a thousand years ago. After modifying it to fit their tastes, the Japanese adopted it as the national female costume of the country.

The kimono is still very much in evidence as the official, formal wear of Japanese women, and is worn regularly at parties, weddings, festivals, and holidays. It is also commonly worn by maids in inns, by geisha, by some cabaret hostesses*, and by shop clerks and office girls on several annual occasions. Elevator girls and maids in large, name hotels also wear kimono on special days, and because of the contrast with their Western surroundings, appear all the more exotic.

There is a provocative mystique surrounding the kimono. Its patterns and colors are closely related to the age of the wearer. The most brilliant colors and elaborate patterns are worn by young, single girls. But such provocative seductiveness is considered inappropriate for women after they marry, and their kimono are more subdued. The

---

*The percentage of cabaret hostesses wearing kimono has been declining since the mid-1960s, when half of them favored the national costume, apparently because of their expense and the complicated steps involved in putting them on. Of the 36,000 hostesses presently working in Tokyo's Ginza district, only around three hundred of them regularly wear kimono, according to kimono materials dealers. These dealers say that nowadays only *mama-sans* (the female managers of cabarets) and the top-earning hostesses wear kimono (one of whom says she spends $100 a day to have a professional dresser come to her apartment to help her don her kimono before leaving for work). As a result of this change, one department store on the Ginza that used to sell materials for 3,500 kimono each day, and devoted two whole floors to their display, now sells two or three a day. The material for a kimono costs from two hundred thousand to five hundred thousand yen (about $1,300 to $3,300).

older the wearer, generally the more conservative the colors and patterns of the kimono.

Young Japanese girls and women today still like the kimono because the sensuous patterns and beautiful materials of which they are made accent their youth and glorify their charms, thereby acting as a powerful stimulant to the male sex.

The yukata, originally an undergarment for the kimono and now used by both men and women as a bathrobe, nightgown, and the national leisure costume, is not only more comfortable and convenient than the kimono, it is also sexier. I think it is one of the most seductive garments a woman can wear.

The summer yukata consists of a single, thin layer of decorated cotton cloth that snuggles the body kimono-fashion, both concealing and revealing the figure at the same time. Its sexiness is considerably heightened by its connection with the bath, bed, and hot-spring resort spas. Traditionally yukata were worn without any undergarments, and there is always the intriguing question of whether the present-day wearer follows tradition.

In winter, a kind of yukata wrap called *dotera* (doe-tay-rah) may be worn over the yukata.

To fully appreciate the role the yukata plays in life in Japan, you must experience it yourself. The intimacy it generates, particularly when you are in a ryokan in a resort noted for its scenic beauty and romantic history, is almost magical.

Both the kimono and the yukata have a remarkable psychological effect on Japanese girls and women. Because of the nature of the two garments, worn wrapped around the body robe-fashion, from ankle to neck, the wearer is forced to move in a restrained and graceful manner. This has a remarkably feminizing influence on the wearer as well as itself presenting an image of charged femininity.

In addition to making the wearer look more feminine, and making it more difficult for her to act in other than a feminine manner without appearing grossly vulgar, the kimono and the yukata are representative of the traditional manners and values of Old Japan, and when they are wearing them the women are strongly affected by this influence.

When the Japanese girl or woman changes from Western dress to a kimono or yukata it is like stepping out of one culture into another. Not only her appearance but her attitude and behavior as well undergo subtle changes.

While most Westerners react favorably to the exotic and sensual attractions of the kimono, they are inclined to regard it as simply too restricting. But its formidability is misleading. The large arm holes give direct access to the area of the breasts, and the skirt of the garment can be flipped open to the waist in a matter of seconds.

The yukata is even more erotic. Although completely concealing, it reveals while covering, and can be opened from top to bottom in one quick motion—or shed completely in two movements.

Many Western visitors to Japan, perhaps out of a sense of embarrassment, are reluctant to wear the yukata even inside their ryokan. This is another of the many times when you are in Japan that you should put aside such feelings and wholeheartedly enter into the spirit of the place and the occasion.

The Sensational Hot-Spring Spas

Japan has more known hot-spring spas than any other country, and hundreds of them have been in use since ancient times. There are over 1,100 spas whose waters have recognized medicinal value.

A number of Japan's best-known cities owe their prominence to hot-springs (Atami, Ito, Unzen, and Beppu among them), and several hundred small towns and communities throughout the ilsands are built around natural hot-springs which serve as their primary economic resource.

Most of the country's famous winter ski resorts, including Zao and Akakura, are built over giant hot-springs which often seem more popular than the adjoining snow-covered slopes.

One of Japan's most spectacular and famous hot-spring resorts is *Noboribetsu* (no-boe-ree-bate-sue) in Hokkaido. Located in a large ravine formed by the Kusurisambetsu River in a section of the Shikotsu-Toya National Park (about an hour and a half train ride from Sapporo), the spa includes eleven large hot-springs. Each of the springs has a complex of inns surrounding it, and a different mineral content, so the visitor can choose the one he or she believes will be the most beneficial—or visit them all!

Mixed-sex bathing is the rule in Noboribetsu, and some of the baths, which look like huge pool-pocked gardens, will accommodate over one hundred bathers at a time without crowding. This is an especially good place for the visitor to get his first taste of mixed bathing because the steam rising up from the pools of hot water keeps visibility in the baths low at all times.

The most popular of the hot-springs near Tokyo are Atami, Hakone, Ito, Nasu, Kinugawa, and Shiobara. Atami, less than an hour from Tokyo by express train, is perched on the side of half of an extinct volcano—the other half collapsed into the sea ages ago—and has dozens of hot-spring inns and hotels. It has long been noted as a honeymoon spot, a hideaway for weekend lovers, and a favorite place to hold company parties.

Hakone, a large district that includes *Ashi-no Ko* (ah-she-no koe) or Hakone Lake, has fourteen spas within its boundaries: Yumoto, Tonosawa, Miyanoshita, Dogashima, Sokokura, Kowakidani, Kiga, Gora, Ubako, Sengokuhara, Ashinoyu, Yunohanazawa, Ohiradai, and Moto-Hakone— all located in areas so superbly scenic that any attempt to describe their settings quickly become redundant with superlatives.

The entire Hakone district lies within the crater of an extinct volcano that measures approximately twenty-five miles in circumference. Inside the crater are several volcanic peaks, two rivers, a great lake, and a total of seventeen communities.

Most of the hot-spring spas of Hakone are perched on the rim or just below the rim of the ancient crater, affording visitors spectacular views of lower mountain ranges, valleys, and gorges. Several of the most noted spa inns and hotels have unobstructed views of the towering pinnacle of Mt. Fuji, which dwarfs everything within two hundred miles.

Hakone is about the same distance from Tokyo as Atami—a little over an hour by train and about ninety minutes by toll turnpike. It is a much larger area than Atami, and offers a larger variety of activities—boating, fishing, water-skiing, and golf courses that are unsurpassed for surrounding scenery.

Beppu (bape-puu), facing the Inland Sea on the northern coast of Kyushu (que-shuu), is the best known of the many hot springs on the southernmost of Japan's four main islands. There are actually eight hot-spring spas in this district, plus a large number of boiling "mud ponds" (called "hells" in Japanese) which have long been used as mud baths for their therapeutic value. One of the most amazing of these "hells" is vermilion in color, maintains a constant temperature of 93 degrees centigrade, and is an estimated five hundred feet deep.

At least one hot-spring spa should be a must on every visitor's itinerary, and you will be shortchanging yourself if you don't spend some time at two or three of the more spectacular ones. A tour devoted exclusively to ten or twenty of Japan's most famous hot springs would be an incomparable experience.

As the term suggests, hot-spring spas are places to go to play and relax. You can pick your spa according to the season (some are high in the mountains, others are at seaside) and according to what you want to do in addition to bathing—play golf, ski, hike, swim, fish, go boating, or just laze the time away in the baths.

You can even pick your spa on the basis of the mineral content of the water, since there are many kinds that are recommended for different things. Wherever you go, a spa is no place to go alone. A companion is absolutely essential to make the experience complete.

Return of the Public Baths

With the coming of affluence to Japan in the 1960s and 1970s, the venerable institution of the *sento* (sin-toe) or public baths went into a rapid decline as new apartments and homes generally had built-in bathtubs and showers. In 1964, the peak year, there were 23,000 *sento* nationwide. By 1987 this had fallen to approximately 11,000.

But the prophets who predicted the total demise of the neighborhood public baths did not take into consideration the entrepreneurial spirit of the bathhouse operators or the long Japanese tradition of bathing as a recreational and social experience as well as a hygiene practice.

A Ministry of Health and Welfare survey shows that the surviving bathhouses are rapidly adding a variety of facilities and services to attract more clients and increase their cash flow. One *sento* in Osaka has a sauna, an "electric bath," an open-air tub on the roof, plus a water slide for children in the main bath area. The bathhouse is so popular people from other neighborhoods drive to it. Tsurunoyu, a *sento* in Tokyo's Koto Ward, features a variety show three times a month. Other bathhouses have workout rooms and aerobic classes, etc.

Given Japan's long history in combining bathing facilities with various forms of pleasure, a much safer prediction would probably be that the *sento* will continue to make a comeback in numbers as well as in variety of services as they redefine their image and role to fit the times. The visitor who wants to experience this aspect of traditional Japan will have no trouble in being directed to a public bath.

The Landscaped Gardens

Japan's landscaped gardens are one of the most distinctive features of the country, and add a special dimension to its enjoyment. No one knows when the art of landscape gardening appeared in Japan, but it was already commonplace in 720 A.D. when the *Chronicles of Japan,* the first history, was compiled—attesting to the existence long before then of a highly civilized style of living and the particular Japanese attachment to beauty in their surroundings.

For untold centuries, the Japanese gave landscaped gardens as much if not more consideration than the homes or buildings they surrounded. They have traditionally been an integral part of temples and shrines and the private homes of the more affluent, with the result that there are uncounted thousands of them beautifying the country.

Many of Japan's most famous landscaped gardens were created by noted Zen tea masters of the day. The garden of the *Chishaku-in* (chee-sha-kuu-een) Temple in Kyoto, for example, was originally laid out by Sen-no Rikyu (1521–1591), regarded as the greatest tea master of all. The celebrated garden of the *Katsura* (kot-sue-rah) Detached Palace in Kyoto was designed by another tea master, Enshu Kobori, whose other gardens include those of the famous Daitoku (die-toe-kuu), Kodai (koe-die), Nanzen (nahn-zen), and Chion (chee-own) Temples.

Among the most noted gardens in Tokyo are Korakuen (koe-rah-kuu-een), Rikugien (ree-kuu-ghee-een), Hyakkaen (h'yahk-kah-een), and Kiyosumi (kee-yoe-sue-me). Two of Tokyo's better-known restaurants, Chinzanso (cheen-zahn-soe) and Hannyaen (hahn-yah-een), both formerly mansions of feudal lords, include equally famous gardens.

National Parks

Because of their exceptional natural beauty, twenty-three large areas of Japan have been designated as national parks, and are regarded as irreplaceable national treasures by the people.

There are five such parks in Hokkaido, made up of volcanoes, hot springs, mountain lakes, and virgin forests. One of these five, *Daisetsuzan* (die-sate-sue-zahn), is the largest park in the country, covering 1,438 square miles. Honshu, the largest and the main island of Japan, has several national parks, including the famous Nikko-Bandai-Asahi, the Fuji-Hakone-Izu, and the Ise-Shima, with their mountains, volcanoes, lakes, rivers, forests, seacoasts, and offshore islets.

Japan's most unusual national park is the *Seto Naikai* (say-toe nie-kie) or Inland Sea, which is bounded by Kyushu, Shikoku, and the southern part of Honshu, and is made up mostly of water. This unbelievably scenic area has been known since ancient times as "A Sight Fit for the Eyes of a King."

Comparatively shallow (up to 120 feet), the Inland Sea is studded with some 950 islands that are mostly pine-tree covered and swarms with a wide variety of colorful sealife. The coastlines formed by the surrounding islands are marked by an incredible number of bays, coves, and inlets, hundreds of white-sand beaches, and an apron of green pine trees, twisted and gnarled from the action of the coastal winds.

Several luxury liners cruise the Inland Sea Park, leaving from Osaka and calling at Kobe, Takamatsu, Beppu, and some of the larger islands in the sea. Life on some of these islands has changed very little since the days of Old Japan, and afford the visitor another rare opportunity to step back in time.

In addition to the national parks, there are also twenty-seven quasi-national parks in Japan, plus over two hundred other parks that are maintained by prefectural governments.

One Vast Museum

A great part of the unusual charm of Japan derives from the presence of so much handicraft art. Until the introduction of industrial machines and modern technology into the country from 1868 onward, Japanese industry was primarily made up of artisans and craftsmen whose work was characterized by a high level of artistic excellence that had been handed down for centuries. The first Westerners to visit Japan often remarked that the whole country was one vast museum of handicraft arts.

The system responsible for the presence of so much

handicraft art in Japan was that of the master and the apprentice. Boys in their early teens or younger were apprenticed to skilled craftsmen for at least ten and sometimes for as long as thirty years. The standards of excellence that resulted from this system, which was guided aesthetically by the Zen concept of restrained natural beauty, were applied to everything the Japanese used in their daily lives, from soup bowls to paper fans.

The impression these handicrafted items make upon the foreign viewer is strongly enhanced by the fact that they are made of natural materials that have an extraordinary bucolic beauty of their own—bamboo, stone, potter's clay, handmade paper, wood, straw, plant fibers, and handworked metals.

Despite the abundance now of machine-made goods (which are functional but have little or no artistic merit), Japan's ancient handicrafts have managed to survive, and in some instances are even more conspicuous today because they stand out from assembly-line products. Items that are still made in the traditional manner include lacquerware, pottery, ceramics, and metal teapots. Such products can invariably be found in every inn and home in the land.

The presence of so much common art, seen also in the structure of the traditional-style homes, ryokan, restaurants, even the finishing and decor of Western buildings, gives off vibrations of naturalness, warmth, sincerity, and refinement that have a tranquilizing, sensual effect on the sensitive viewer.

The Traditions of Traveling

The Japanese of old, perhaps more than any other people, celebrated the beauty and the other attractions of their country in deed as well as in word. Their love of travel goes back to prehistoric times and is regarded as a national trait. Japanese literature compiled in the eighth century A.D. is replete with references to people traveling about the country, in groups and singly, for just about every purpose imaginable.

Buddhist monks had a great deal to do with popularizing travel in Japan. As early as the seventh century, when much of central and all of northern Honshu and Hokkaido were wild frontiers inhabited by *Ainu* (aye-nuu) tribesmen, Buddhist monks were making their way by foot to the remotest parts of the islands. Seeking out places of extraordinary beauty—on hills, in valleys and virtually inaccessible gorges, and on the highest mountains—they built thousands of temples (many of which still exist today), where they often spent the rest of their days in religious and artistic pursuits.

Shintoist priests were also great travelers because there is hardly a nob, hill, mountain, or attractive spot in between that does not have its Shinto shrine dating back hundreds of years. Still today there are over 140,000 listed Shinto shrines in the country.

As the greater of all these Buddhist temples and Shintoist shrines gained fame, usually through the extraordinary accomplishments of their founders or later heads, they began to attract followers who regularly made pilgrimages to visit them.

More important in the development of travel in Japan at this early date, however, was an action taken by the imperial government. In the latter part of the seventh century, the settled areas of the country were divided into provinces which were grouped together into "circuits" *(do)* that were assigned to supervisory officials and tax collectors. Each year these government officials, with retinues of various sizes, set out on these circuits—with the officials usually on horseback and their staffs walking—to make their rounds.

To facilitate traveling to the outlying districts and provinces of the country, the government developed and maintained a network of roads leading from the capital in Kyoto to every provincial village and town in the country.

Because the traffic was on foot, food stands, inns, and other facilities were established at short intervals along all of these national roads, giving Japan a roadway system that was comparable to the ones developed by the Chinese, the Romans, and the Incas.

The most famous of Japan's roads was known as the *To Kai Do* (toe kie doe), also written as Tokaido, or Eastern Sea Route, which passed through the provinces between Kyoto and the Kanto Plain (where Tokyo now stands), following the coastline except where it crossed peninsulas jutting out into the Pacific Ocean.

As the centuries passed, the traffic on these national roads continued to grow in volume and importance—particularly along the *To Kai Do* after 1192, when Kamakura just south of Tokyo became the capital city of the new shogunate system of government administration.

But this was nothing compared to what was to happen in the early 1600s, after Ieyasu Tokugawa became shogun and moved the shogunate government to his castle in Edo (present-day Tokyo). Ieyasu's grandson (and successor) issued an edict in 1638 that thereafter over two hundred of the country's provincial feudal lords, known as *Daimyo* (dime-yoe) or "Great Names," would keep their families in Edo and themselves spend every other year there in attendance at the shogun's court.

Each of the lords, along with a retinue of warriors and retainers, was thus required to travel on foot from their fiefs to Edo every other year. These troupes of marching lords and their retainers were known as *Daimyo Gyoretsu* (dime-yoe g'yoe-rate-sue) or "Processions of the Lords."

Each day these columns of lords, ladies, and warriors marched approximately thirty miles, stopping over every night at "post stations" interspersed along the way. There were fifty-three such post stations between the imperial capital in Kyoto and the shogunate capital in Edo. (These stations were immortalized by the great woodblock print artist Hiroshige, also known for his "Thirty-Six Views of Mt. Fuji." The prints were so common during the latter part of the Tokugawa period that they were often used as wrapping paper, which is said to be how the first ones reached Europe, where they came to be regarded as outstanding works of art.)

Maeda, the richest of the provincial lords, maintained four large mansions in Edo with a total staff of some 10,000 persons. When he came to Edo for his turn at the shogun's court, he brought several hundred additional warriors and retainers with him.

The samurai warriors of each lord were richly garbed in brilliant uniforms. Lesser retainers were dressed in apparel denoting their occupation and position. All were marked with the identifying crest of the clan to which they belonged. The lord himself usually rode in an enclosed palanquin carried by teams of men. Some of his warriors were mounted on horses; the rest of the procession marched in rigidly prescribed formation, preceded and flanked by guards.

It is estimated that ten percent of the annual income of the provincial lords was used on these yearly journeys to and from Edo—in a system that continued for over two hundred years and was undoubtedly the most distinctive and colorful feature of Japanese life for these many generations. (For more on the Processions of the Lords see The Traditions of Hospitality, Chapter VI.)

Despite many checkpoints on the roads connecting Edo with provincial cities, especially during the Tokugawa period, voluminous records show large numbers of people were constantly on the move. One of the highest adventures of this period was to travel the *To Kai Do* from Edo to Kyoto, and one of the first travel books written in Japan chronicles the misadventures of two rather irresponsible men from Edo named Yajiro and Kitahachi, making their way down the famous road, stopping at teahouses and inns along the way, getting in and out of trouble. Theirs was the original "road show," duplicated in the 1940s by Bob Hope and Bing Crosby in their famous "Road to" series of films.

In addition to the processions of the clan lords, shogunate officials, and representatives of the imperial court who were constantly on the road during the Tokugawa era, many other travelers, including priests and monks, peddlers, gamblers, entertainers, poets, masterless samurai, and merchants, used this extensive network of roads on a daily basis.

This tradition of traveling within Japan has continued. Annual student trips around the country are a part of the national educational system. Virtually every company in the country sponsors annual company trips as recreational outings for it employees. Associations of farmers and other rural organizations sponsor domestic trips for their members every year. Urban residents visit their ancestral towns or villages regularly—at least once a year if their parents still live there. Literally millions of other people make short-to-long trips each year to visit hot-spring spas or beaches or to go skiing or mountain-climbing. Pilgrimages to distant shrines and temples are also a popular activity in modern-day Japan. Honeymoon trips are a major industry.

All of this activity supports what is probably the most efficient hospitality industry in the world, and is the primary reason why traveling in Japan is so convenient and pleasant for visitors from abroad.

Touring by Car

It is now entirely feasible for foreign visitors who want to see Japan close-up to tour the country by car. There is an outstanding network of toll expressways, well marked by international signs. Good travel maps are plentiful, as are roadside services, from restaurants and toilets to motels, hotels, and inns.

The main thing car-tourers should keep in mind is to thoroughly familiarize themselves with Japan's highway signs and road maps, so they can travel from place to place with confidence, and not constantly be trying to figure out where they are and how they can get to their next destination.

Japan has several special advantages that have contributed to its emergence as one of the world's best leisure-time motoring countries. The first of these is that literally thousands of scenic and recreational areas have been developed and famous for hundreds of years. Second is that no matter where you are in the islands, you cannot be more than a short drive from not one or a few but dozens of places of historical, scenic, or recreational interest. There are hundreds of "Leisure Villages" and "Inland Isles" featuring villas, motels, drive-ins, service stations, and other facilities in some of the most scenic areas on the globe.

Rental cars are available from several large American and Japanese companies, as well as from joint U.S.-Japanese firms. Keep in mind that you need an international driver's license before you can rent a car in Japan. Such licenses are easy to obtain in your home country.

A word of warning, however. The streets and highways near Japan's major cities become jam-packed on holidays and weekends. You should definitely take this into consideration in your planning.

CHAPTER V

Bunka No Toge
Crossing the Cultural Barriers

A Rose Is Not a Rose

In Japan a rose is a *bara-no hana* (bah-rah-no hah-nah), which is "rose" by another name, but with roses as well as other things in Japan, the name is often where the similarity stops. Virtually everything you see, hear, eat, and otherwise experience physically in Japan today must be interpreted in its proper "Japanese" context.

One of the more conspicuous examples of what you see not being what you are supposed to get is the use of the English language in print advertisements, as product names, slogans, and various other labels.

It is natural for the visitor to look at English as English, and to expect it to make sense. This is one of the first and most common mistakes foreigners make in cross-cultural communications with the Japanese. In Japan, English is not used as just English. It is also used to create moods, as an exotic ingredient, to exude sophistication, to help the Japanese feel less provincial and more cosmopolitan, more international.

When used in this manner English does not have to

remain true to its original English-language meaning. That often is of no consequence whatsoever. The name of one popular soft drink immediately comes to mind: *Pocari Sweat* (poe-cah-ree). *Pocari* means nothing to the foreign visitor, but *sweat* is not something any English speaker would ever associate with a refreshing drink. (*Pocari* doesn't mean anything in Japanese, either. It was chosen as a brand name because it "sounds good" to Japanese ears.)

Many of the uses of English in Japan turn out to be humorous (from the viewpoint of foreigners). A popular toilet paper goes by the brand name of "My Fanny." I would like to believe that the creative expert who came up with this name understood the humor involved, but that is doubtful.

Even more pervasive and much more important in how visitors perceive Japan is the difference in the way Westerners and Japanese view human relations, including normal daily communication, the difference in priorities, the rationale for their actions, and so on.

Maintaining harmonious human relations is so important in Japan that this need has traditionally determined how the Japanese communicate with each other. The language is constructed and used first to maintain and enhance harmony and favorable relations, and second to communicate information.

This form of social ethics and etiquette is of course responsible for the famed ceremonial behavior and politeness of the Japanese—which is seen as very positive from the outside, but makes communicating with the Japanese very delicate, difficult, and often impossible in terms of Western logic.

The Japanese are, of course, acutely aware of the delicate nature of their interpersonal relations system, because it causes them more trouble and more frustration than it does foreigners. The foreigner is not always automatically expected to know and abide by Japanese rules of behavior, and in normal social situations can get by with only routine polite behavior. The Japanese themselves, however, have no such out. They are expected to follow every subtle twist and turn of special language use, body language, and over-all attitude in all their dealings with each other.

Japanese attitudes toward foreigners have changed in recent years and are changing still. As their economic and political status rises, they have begun to expect more of foreigners—but more so in business than in the travel industry. In fact, there is a separate set of rules and behavior for travelers in Japan.

Foreign businessmen in Japan today, particularly those who are selling instead of buying, have to be much more knowledgeable and skilled in conducting (and that is the proper word) their relations with their clients, prospects, and government officials. This especially applies to for-eigners called on to sell advertising or other services to Japanese companies, since the products are intangibles.*

While visitors are spared the more demanding social re-quirements in their own personal behavior in Japan, the degree and depth of their enjoyment of the Japanese life-style is greatly influenced by the extent that they can avoid judging everything they see by Western standards and get into the cultural spirit of things.

Breaking Out of Your Cocoon

The biggest problem facing Western tourists visiting Japan is not the language barrier or unfamiliarity with the Japa-

---

*For a detailed analysis of the business culture in Japan, see the author's *Japanese Etiquette and Ethics in Business* (Passport Books) and *How to Do Business with the Japanese* (NTC Business Books).

nese lifestyle. It is the limitations and restrictions imposed on them by their own culture. The visitor who has the best time in Japan is the one who can shed several layers of cultural skin and really get involved in the Japanese scene.

One of the most common daily experiences is, of course, eating. The visitor who refuses, for example, to try using *hashi* (hah-she), or chopsticks, is not only missing out on a new experience but some fun—as simple and as innocuous as this action may seen to be.

The challenge is for you to be fully conscious of the importance of letting yourself go and personally experiencing new things, new ways of sitting, eating, bathing, and so on.

An unbecoming number of Westerners who visit Japan expect—and often demand—the same kind and quality of accommodations and food that they are used to at home. As mentioned earlier, many of these people are so afraid to try anything new that they do little more than glimpse Japan in passing. Their trip abroad is little more than a change in geographical location.

Choosing a Western-style hotel over a *ryokan* inn, for example, just for the sake of familiarity and convenience, means that you automatically give up one of the most distinctive, interesting, and educational experiences in Japan.

Just making this choice requires a kind and quality of courage that many people no longer have. It is also unfortunately the kind of choice that the majority of people planning trips to Japan do not consider seriously or at all.

The blame for this does not belong entirely to travelers. For many decades, the travel industry has deliberately designed and constructed hotels and other tourist-oriented facilities to be essentially the same as the facilities they are used to at home—the idea being to offer travelers familiar accommodations and services . . . *to make sure they are comfortable and have a good time.*

The fact that this approach removes much of the adventure, fun, and benefit from the foreign experience is glossed over lightly by the travel industry, which takes the position that travelers can have their cake and eat it too (enjoy the comforts of home while having a marvelous time in a foreign country). A great deal of foreign travel thus becomes a one-dimensional affair, instead of the rich, cross-cultural experience that comes only from "going native."

Just as you cannot know or enjoy the taste of a mango or papaya without eating one, you cannot know or appreciate the pleasures of other lifestyles without physically experiencing them. Physical experience is totally different from intellectual experience—which, again, one can have from viewing a videotape.

Everyone who travels abroad should make a firm commitment in advance to go beyond the Western-style hotels and restaurants, and get away from the paved paths neatly laid out by the travel industry. This commitment should include learning some of the language, learning something about the history of the country, eating the food, and participating in living experiences.

I recall one 27-year-old American a few years ago who came to Japan as a tourist on vacation, intending to stay for two weeks. He was determined to see and experience the "real Japan" (which, I'm delighted to say, he read about in one of my books). To do so, he skipped Tokyo and went directly to a small fishing village near the end of Izu Peninsula.

There were no hotels or inns in the village. He wandered around until he found an old man sitting outside his home. Using a Japanese-English conversational dictionary, he managed to convey to the aged man that he wanted to stay in the village for a few days for no reason other than to enjoy the ambience of the life of its people.

The old man led him to a nearby house, the home of the head of the village, and in a few minutes he was invited in for tea and sweetened bean cakes. The wife of the village head and her young daughter, the only ones home, discussed the situation with the old man. Within a few minutes—with the aid of one of the girl's schoolbooks—they were able to tell the visitor that he could stay at their home.

A week later the man telephoned his employer in the U.S., quit his job, and spent the rest of the summer and fall in the village. He went out with the fishermen. He attended village meetings. He taught English to the children and wives of the fishermen. He went to weddings and funerals. On his way back to the U.S. he stopped over in Tokyo and told me it was the best time, the most satisfying time, and the best learning experience he had ever had.

Of course, this kind of spur-of-the-moment decision is beyond most of us, but it epitomizes the idea of what true cross-cultural experience is all about.

Even one day away from a scheduled trip, spent in a private home or visiting a school or some small village, can be the highlight of a trip, overshadowing the spectacular luxury of a great international hotel, the awe and appreciation inspired by a huge monument, temple, shrine, or castle. The simple secret of getting a lot out of a trip to Japan is to step outside your own cultural cocoon and live in the Japanese environment for as long as possible.

Getting Set for New Sensations

The first step in preparing for a sojourn inside "real Japan"—after you have made the commitment to do so—is to begin a crash course in the study of the Japanese language. This book (see *A Little Language Goes a Long Way*) will get you started. Another one that I recommend (without any embarrassment at all) is my own *Japanese in Plain English* (Passport Books). In addition to that book, I also recommend that you get a Japanese-language video or cassette tape. One of the best (and I think the most interesting) Japanese-language videos is called "Living Japanese," which is produced by Cross Cultural Communications in Tokyo.

"Living Japanese"—in the sense of both the living language and the Japanese lifestyle—does two things. It teaches the language and shows the life and work styles of the Japanese in a broad and comprehensive manner.

There are many other very good language books on Japan—one of the handiest being the conversational dictionary the young American used during his stay in the Izu Peninsula fishing village. Its title is *English-Japanese Conversation Dictionary*, written by the late Oreste and Elize Vaccari, who were pioneers in the publishing of Japanese-language teaching materials.

The second step, which can be taken simultaneously, is to get several other particular books on Japan that will round out your Japan orientation and provide you with specific information for day-to-day use. Since food is a daily necessity (as well as a major expense if you do not know where to eat in Japan), I recommend that the next book you buy be *Eating Cheap in Japan*, written by Kimiko Nagasawa and Camy Condon, and published by Shufunotomo.

Another valuable little book that is filled with useful Japanese-language sentences and hundreds of useful facts about everyday life in Japan, from using telephones and post offices to buying train tickets, is *Gaijin's Guide* (guyjeen), written by Janet Ashby and published by *The Japan Times*.

A very valuable *big* book is (again) one of mine: *The Japan Almanac*, which is an encyclopedic reader on things Japanese, covering some nine hundred topics that range from art, business, crafts, energy, fishing, gardening, history, martial arts and other sports to women and zen. Designed to be a one-volume reference on Japan, the book answers virtually all of the common questions one might have about Japan, plus several hundred others—included because they are unusually interesting and/or useful.

Going through these books will take several days (the smaller ones you will want to take with you on your trip), and each additional hour that you spend studying the Japanese language will contribute that much more to your enjoyment and the benefits that you will gain from your trip. It has often occurred to me that not being able to converse with someone, even on a very basic level, is something like taking a shower in a rubber suit that covers you from head to foot. You don't get the feel of the water.

The next step is to actually plan your trip, either on your own or with the help of a travel agent. If you want to plan your own trip, contact the nearest office of the Japan National Tourist Organization (JNTO). (For a list of the overseas offices of JNTO see the back of this book.) Tell the JNTO staff by phone or letter what you would like to see and do in Japan. They will send you all kinds of detailed current information. This includes pamphlets and booklets that describe many special services and facilities designed for non-tour-group travel in Japan.

The Sense of Safety

One of the great advantages of traveling on your own in Japan, either by yourself or with a friend or friends, is that you do not have to worry about personal security. Japan is one of the safest countries in the world. Incidents of public violence, muggings, purse-snatching, and the like are very, very rare. Women (and children) of all nationalities come and go as they please in Japan, day or night, in what could be described as the most disreputable parts of cities, without fearing for their safety. Of course one should exercise sensible caution just to avoid becoming the victim of some rare incident, but there is a great feeling of relief and comfort in the sure knowledge that you do not have to be constantly on guard against a threat of violence.

If you prefer to go to a travel agent for your arrangements, fine. They can be a great help to you at no cost (since their commissions come from the travel industry services). But if you want more than a canned package tour you must be willing and able to work with the agent to get what you want. This means, of course, that you have to *know* what your options are—that you can stay in modern hotel-type youth hostels or folk lodges as well as in luxury tourist hotels; that you can get excellent food in a *shokudo* (show-kuu-doe) at one-third to one-tenth of what it costs in a name hotel; that you can arrange to stay with Japanese families, etc.

Perhaps the most important thing in visiting Japan on an arranged tour is to make sure you have programmed in a goodly number of personal experiences to balance the sightseeing (which should be a minor part of your overall trip), along with lots of free time to do things on your own and to react to opportunities that invariably arise (to go somewhere not scheduled, to spend time with people, to stop running and smell the *bara*).

Of course, this is the kind of thing that is often incompatible with the travel industry system, which is designed to operate more like a space mission, with everything and everybody following prescribed moves. Some of the experiences and pleasures you can have in Japan might send you into orbit, but it is better to get there on your own instead of riding on a fast-moving rocket that someone else is controlling.

In summary, the challenge in getting the most out of traveling abroad today is to take time to prepare yourself for the trip, to either slow the system down or get off it entirely, and to include as much as possible of the personal and human touch in the experience.

Locking In the Memories

An ideal approach, which appears to be beyond the control of most of us, would be to travel to Japan by air and return by sea. There is no way in the near future that air or space travel could begin to compare with the special ambience and pleasures of shipboard travel no matter which way you are going—to or from.

But over and above the inherent benefits of taking a slow ship home (besides totally avoiding the debilitation of time-lag) is the opportunity it gives one to make the transition from Japan to your home country over a period of several days instead of hours, during which you are in between cultures and can contemplate and enjoy over and over again all of your best Japan experiences.

When you go both to and from even a distant country in just a few hours it takes away much of the prior anticipation and following contemplation. As we all know, in many things in life anticipating is often better than the real thing. Particularly in the case of a visit to a foreign country, no matter how intense the experience, it tends to lose something when we almost literally step out of one culture into another. The new and different experiences have not had time to become an integral part of us.

For many people, the rapid transition from Japan back

to their own home or office leaves them feeling as though the trip was just a dream that they could have imagined (at no expense and without the physical problems that come from abruptly changing time zones). Fortunately there are several ways besides going home by sea to counter this illusion of reality becoming unreal. But if you *can* force yourself to stop the world long enough to take an extra ten days or two weeks before re-entering your own sphere, do it. The benefits will enrich the rest of your life.

CHAPTER VI

Kogu No Dento
The Traditions of Hospitality

The Traveler as a Very Important Person

I do not know of any country in the world that treats travelers with more kindness, courtesy, generosity, respect, and all-around good service than Japan. The Japanese commonly refer to travelers as *O'kyaku* (oh-kyah-kuu) or "guests." And travelers are treated as special guests, with a type and quality of service generally reserved for Very Important People in the West.

The special kind of treatment afforded travelers in Japan came about for a number of reasons. One of the tenets of Buddhism, in which Japanese culture is steeped, is that all travelers are to be treated with the utmost respect and kindness. The Japanese have thus been conditioned in the "Good Samaritan" concept for more than a thousand years.

Shintoism, which is Japan's indigenous religion and predates Buddhism by well over a thousand years, teaches unselfish respect and service to other people.

It was, however, the appearance of the feudal shogunate system in 1192 A.D. and the subsequent proliferation of the

Samurai warrior class with their *Bushido* (buu-she-doe) "Way of the Warrior" ethics and practices that was the most important in shaping the attitudes and behavior of Japanese in all areas of their lives, including that of traveling.

The codes of behavior established by the shogunate government for the ruling Samurai class were very, very specific and very strict. The behavior and etiquette demanded of the lower classes was somewhat less restrictive, but was nevertheless very precise, especially when it came to their interaction with the Samurai class. Any breach of etiquette was a serious offense; some, in fact, called for the death sentence (which was often carried out on the spot by arrogant Samurai warriors).

The shogunate action that put the finishing touches on the attitude of the Japanese toward travelers occurred in 1635. In that year, the ruling Tokugawa shogun ordered all of the larger of the some 270 provincial lords around the country, known as *Daimyo* (dime-yoe) or "Great Names," to establish residences in Edo, the shogunate capital, to keep their families there at all times, and to spend every other year in Edo in attendance at the shogun's court.

The edict specified when each of the *Daimyo* would travel to Edo, the route they were to take, the number of retainers and warriors they were authorized to bring with them, the kinds of weapons they could carry, and even where they would stop at night. The number of overall retainers was based on the size and wealth of the particular fief.

The reasons for this edict were political: to in effect keep the families of the ambitious *Daimyo* as virtual hostages, to keep the *Daimyo* themselves away from their fiefs half of the time and in Edo where they would have less chance of plotting an insurrection against the shogun, and to keep them from building up the wealth they would need to raise a rebellion against the shogunate.

Thus began a system that was to become one of the most important political, economic, and social activities in Japan until the fall of the Tokugawa Shogunate in 1867. Virtually all travel in Japan during those long decades was by foot—only members of the imperial court in Kyoto, high personages in the Tokugawa Shogunate, some warriors, and messengers were allowed to ride horseback or be carried in palanquins, and there was no wheeled passenger transportation.

This meant that the various *Daimyo* were on the road for varying lengths of time—from a few days for those who were nearest Edo, to several weeks for those whose fiefs were in the farthest reaches of the kingdom. These troops of feudal lords, retainers, and warriors had the absolute right-of-way when they were on the road. Ordinary travelers were required to leave the road, move several yards off, and bow down to the ground while a procession was passing. (In the 1860s a party of foreigners out horseback riding near Yokohama failed to make way for a Daimyo procession. They were immediately attacked by the sword-wielding Samurai guards. One of them was cut down, and the others barely escaped with their lives.)

The inauguration of this system, known as *Kotai Sankin* (koe-tie sahn-keen) or "alternate attendance," resulted in one of the greatest construction booms ever to occur in any country up to that time. Thousands of new inns were built along all of the great walking roads that led to Edo from the provinces. Many of the processions included two hundred to five hundred people or more, requiring several inns to accommodate them. Within a very few years, Japan had the world's largest network of travelers' inns and Japanese-style hotels—a position it probably still holds today, despite the proliferation of motels in the U.S.

In addition to resulting in the rapid development of a vast network of travel facilities, the institution of the *Kotai*

Sankin system was to have a profound effect on the attitude and manners of the people employed in this new industry. The *Daimyo* were absolute rulers in their own domains, with the power of life and death over their subjects. This power accompanied them when they were on the road and could be applied to any commoner they encountered.

The Samurai warriors belonging to each of the fief clans were trained to perfection, fiercely loyal to their lords, and extraordinarily sensitive to any breach of prescribed etiquette toward themselves or their masters—and they had the authority to instantly attack and cut down any offender.

The behavior of the Samurai as well as the commoners during this long period was carefully prescribed, much of it in detailed written form and so precise, formal, and ceremonial that Miss Manners would have been considered an untutored barbarian.

The innkeepers, maids, and others involved in providing accommodations and services to the processions of the *Daimyo*, already well behaved from centuries of conditioning under the Samurai class, and already extraordinarily solicitous about the comfort and welfare of officials, superiors, and travelers, were required to follow even more explicit rules of behavior and to provide an even finer level of service for their lordly guests.

The penalty for faulty or indifferent service to the lords and their ranking retainers was far more serious than the loss of a tip. This, combined with their own conditioned response to treating customers as honored guests, raised the level of service in Japan's lodging business well above what existed anywhere else in the world.

This tradition of service still prevails in Japan's lodging industry in particular, and has been extended pretty much across the board to the entire travel industry, from its airlines and passenger ships to its tourist-oriented restaurants. Thus the traveler in Japan today, regardless of social status, falls heir to a tradition of service and hospitality that is unique.

After a few trips on Japan Air Lines or All-Nippon Airways, for example, it is extremely difficult to accept and be satisfied with the attitudes and behavior of Western flight attendants. The contrast is shocking.

These same traditions of service and hospitality are not limited to the transportation, lodging, and restaurant industries. They are characteristic of the Japanese at large, and are an important part of the attraction of life in Japan.

Hotel Heaven

Despite my advice to first-time visitors to Japan to take advantage of the opportunity to directly experience the traditional Japanese lifestyle by staying in *ryokan*, Western-style hotels are an important and impressive facet of the Japanese hospitality industry.

Taking all factors into consideration, the ideal approach is for the visitor to spend the first two or three days in Japan, and perhaps the last two or three as well, in Western-style hotels, putting up at choice Japanese inns in the interim. This gives the visitor time to rest up from the trip in familiar and comfortable surroundings and to be better prepared physically and emotionally to enjoy a totally different kind of experience in a traditional setting.

Japan's top hotels are in a class by themselves. They are, in fact, an outgrowth of the special luxury inns that were designed and reserved exclusively for the *Daimyo* lords and their chief retainers who had to spend so much of their lives on the road during the Tokugawa Shogunate period.

Each of the hundreds of stopovers on the roads leading to Edo had three classes of inns—the top class, called *Honjin* (hoan-jeen) which was for Very Important People, a second class called *Waki Honjin* (wah-kee hoan-jeen), or "Annex Honjin," for lower-ranking officials and personages, and finally the *hatago* (hah-tah-go) inns that accommodated ordinary travelers.

These luxurious *Honjin* were the predecessors of Japan's present-day luxury-class Western-style hotels, such as the Imperial, the Okura, the Akasaka Prince, and the Ana Hotel. In addition to the usual rooms, suites, conference rooms, and meeting halls, these hotels have anywhere from half a dozen to twenty or more restaurants on their premises, shopping arcades of fifteen to thirty or more individual shops, business service centers, travel agency offices, airline offices, bookshops, drugstores, and more.

Japan's top hotels are major social and entertainment centers, being used for numerous occasions such as weddings and receptions, and offering a variety of cultural and folk exhibits, nightclub-type shows and (in the case of the Imperial) theatrical performances.

While Japan's leading first-class hotels do not offer a new kind of experience, they are often a conspicuous improvement on an old experience, and they are certainly representative of modern-day Japan in all its sophisticated high-tech glory. (Not having to tip bellboys and other service staff in the hotels is another attractive point.)

Besides its internationally famous luxury hotels, Japan has an amazing number of first-class hotels that cater to the traveling public, along with another huge number of so-called businessmen's hotels, which are primarily designed for the hundreds of thousands of Japanese businessmen who are constantly traveling within the country and can't affort to, don't want to, or don't need to stay in a prestigious hotel for their image.

These businessmen's hotels are generally *just* hotels, with smaller rooms at one-half to one-fourth of the rates charged by the international hotels. They have all of the essentials (baths, showers, restaurants, laundry service), and are located near transportation terminals and business districts. They are also becoming more and more popular with foreign tourists and businessmen.

An important consideration in booking one of the first-class hotels is to find out where they are located in relation to primary transportation terminals, shopping areas, and entertainment districts. In Tokyo, for example, there are four areas where the main luxury and first-class hotels are concentrated: the downtown area (Hibiya-Ginza-Marunouchi), the Akasaka-Toranomon area, the West Shinjuku area, and the Shinagawa area.

If you want to be closer in and near major business, shopping, and entertainment areas at the same time, you will choose one of the Hibiya-Ginza-Marunouchi hotels (Tokyo Prince, Imperial, or Palace in the first-class or luxury category, or the Dai-Ichi, Ginza Tokyu, or Shiba Park Hotel if you are seeking more moderately priced accommodations).

In the Akasaka-Toronomon area, adjoining Government Center, the American Embassy, a major geisha inn and nightclub district, and only five to ten minutes from the Ginza and downtown areas, you have the Akasaka Prince, New Otani, Akasaka Tokyu, Capital Tokyu, and, up on a hill across the street from the U.S. Embassy, the famed Okura Hotel. Midway between these two areas is the spectacular Ana Hotel, which is part of the huge Ark Hills complex that includes adjoining executive apartments. This area is also only moments from Roppongi, one of the city's most popular entertainment and restaurant districts, where there are also a number of first-class hotels, including the Roppongi Prince.

In Shinjuku, which is some thirty to forty minutes from downtown, and is a major city in its own right with department stores, a huge concentration of shops, restaurants, and entertainment spots, there is the Tokyo Hilton International, the Keio Plaza, the Century Hyatt, the Washington, and the Shinjuku Prince. Since Shinjuku has become a major business center, these hotels are also popular among foreign businessmen visiting Tokyo.

The fourth major hotel district in Tokyo, Shinagawa, is about the same distance south of the center of Tokyo as Shinjuku is west. It is therefore only twenty to thirty minutes from the downtown area (as well as from most other major centers in Tokyo), but it is not in or immediately adjacent to major shopping or entertainment centers. Hotels in this area are the Pacific Meridien, the Takanawa Prince, the New Takanawa Hotel, and the Shinagawa Prince Hotel.

Other first-class hotels that are outside these districts but still within central Tokyo are the Grand Palace in Iidabashi and the Miyako Hotel Tokyo in Shiroganedai, near Meguro Station. The Sunshine Prince Hotel in Ikebukuro is in a category by itself. It is located in the Sunshine City Building, the tallest building in Japan, with hundreds of shops, restaurants, offices, and other services in the same huge complex.

There are so many businessmen's hotels in Tokyo that you can just about pick the spot you would like to be in or near, and there will be anywhere from a few to dozens of available choices. Some of the better-known ones: Ginza Dai-ei Hotel, Mitsui Urban Hotel (Ginza), Takanawa Tobu Hotel, Hotel Ibis (Roppongi), Hotel Sunroute (Shibuya), Shibuya Tokyu Inn, Hotel Listel Shinjuku, Hotel Sunroute Ikebukuro, and the Juraku Hotel (Ochanomizu).

The Inn Experience

There are over 100,000 *ryokan* inns still operating in Japan (which is about the size of the state of Montana in the U.S. and is so mountainous only about twenty percent of the total area is inhabited). Of this immense number, some two thousand have been designated by the Japan National Tourist Organization as having facilities suitable for foreign guests, which usually means central heating, air-conditioning, Western style toilets, and private baths—for those visitors who choose not to let it all hang out in group baths.

The traditional Japanese inn encompasses most of the fine arts and crafts that are among the highest achievements of Japanese culture. It is designed to be aesthetically pleasing to the senses, tranquilizing to the mind and spirit, seductive in its image and feel, physically comfortable (Japanese-style comfort, of course), and both refreshing and invigorating.

The *ryokan* is made of natural materials that are totally compatible with the environment and its occupants, with wood being the main ingredient. The skill of the architect, the carpenter, and the landscape gardener are immediately evident.

As soon as you step into the *genkan* (gane-kahn) entrance foyer of an inn you go back in time—a hundred years, two hundred and fifty years, even half a millennium. The polished wooden porch and hallways, the *tatami* (tah-tah-me) reed-mat floors, the thick sliding wall panels and the thin rice-paper sliding doors, the *tokonoma* (toe-koe-no-mah) beauty alcove, the wall scrolls, the beautiful woods, the hot baths . . . all have remained basically unchanged for many generations.

Also unchanged is the lifestyle carried on within the inns. From the moment you step up on the entrance landing, minus your street shoes, your lifestyle is also changed. The first thing the newly arrived guest does is change into a *yukata* (yuu-kah-tah), the light cotton kimono-like robe that serves as casual wear as well as sleepwear. This is followed by tea, which is usually accompanied by tiny squares of sweetened beanjam.

The next traditional step is either the family-size hot bath or the *Oburo* (oh-buu-roe) or "big bath," which may accommodate anywhere from a dozen or so to twenty or thirty people (some combination inn/hotels have baths that will accommodate up to a hundred or more people at a time). For a detailed discussion of the pleasures and benefits of the Japanese bath, particularly mixed-sex bathing, see Chapter IX.

Back in your room following a scrub-down fore and aft and a good soaking in the pool (most inn baths can hardly be called "tubs"), you may have lunch or dinner, depending on the time of day, go out for a stroll if the weather is pleasant, have a party, or whatever.

The special ambience of the Japanese inn is a combination of its architecture, building materials, interior decoration, sparse, classically designed furnishings, and an intimacy that is totally lost in a Western-style hotel where the individual rooms are separated by solid walls and heavy doors that are usually kept locked. In contrast to the very private cell-like design and atmosphere of the Western hotel, the Japanese inn gives the feeling of shared intimacy, somewhat like one feels in a private home but much more intensely felt because you are sharing the intimacy with friends and strangers instead of family.

The sliding room-doors of the Japanese inn are never locked—they are not lockable. The interior room dividers—those made of white, almost gossamer-thin rice paper—are translucent and admit the slightest sound, including heavy breathing.

The intimacy of the Japanese inn is sensually exciting, and is a significant part of the pleasure of staying at an inn. Inn maids routinely enter rooms without knocking or calling out—not with any deliberate intention of catching you in a state of undress or engaged in any intimate activity, but simply because it is an age-old custom.

There is, in fact, no word for privacy in the Japanese language. The concept has not been totally alien in the Japanese culture, but it has had such a low order of priority there was obviously no need to name it. Whole families, extended families, and work-groups customarily lived in common rooms, the larger work-groups sometimes in barracks-like settings.

In present-day Japan there is a great deal of personal privacy in the homes of the more affluent, with parents having a private bedroom and children having their own rooms. But it is one of the prime tenets of Japanese business management that even ranking personnel are generally not isolated in private offices. Managers up to the *bucho* (buu-choe) class, which is the equivalent of a vice president in larger companies, share a large open room with everyone else in the division.

The Japanese contention is that it is natural and desirable for people to live and work in close intimacy because mutual understanding, close cooperation, and teamwork are the foundations of society. This belief, with all of its ramifications, especially applies to inns because they are regarded in the Japanese scheme of things as a major part of the pleasure trades (see Chapter XI, "Pleasures of the Night").

In other words, the inn is not just a place to sleep. It is a place to enjoy, to have fun—and then sleep to refresh yourself so you can have more fun the next day. If you think about this concept for a while, and fully understand it, you will be able to get a lot more out of your stay in a Japanese inn.

Western travelers, unfortunately, tend to compare the customs, facilities, and services of the Japanese inn with a Western hotel. The inn often gets low marks because they are comparing pears and apples. No matter how hard you strain, a pear is not going to taste like an apple. The point is to recognize the pear as a pear and savor its special taste and qualities to the fullest.

My best memories of Japan—and I would wager the best memories of most foreign residents and visitors alike—are of experiences that took place in Japanese inns—and not all of these experiences were in the prone position.

One of the most vivid of these memories took place in an inn overlooking the banks of a river near the small city of Seki in the foothills southwest of Nagoya. I was in Seki on a business trip and was invited to lunch by the cutlery manufacturer I was calling on. The inn we went to was several hundred years old. It was situated on a rise that was high enough to afford a view of the river, but not high enough to miniaturize the scene.

We where shown to a room that provided the best view of the river, and served drinks and fresh seafood. The setting was superb; the beauty of the inn was intoxicating; the service was classic Japanese; the food was delicious. For two hours we ate, talked, admired the scenery, and absorbed the total ambience of the experience to its fullest measure.

The only thing that could have improved on the experience would have been to share it with a female companion. But that is another story—or I should say, many stories.

Again unfortunately, many Westerners do not know how to fully let go and enjoy themselves. They are so conditioned to work and to regarding themselves and everything in the world seriously that they have lost the childlike ability to give their intellectual self time off, to suspend it actually, to let their human senses take over, to exercise and stretch themselves to their limits. The Japanese inn is designed for this kind of sensual pleasuring. It sets the mood and provides the place. You just have to recognize what it is offering you, and take advantage of it.

Some inns are much better for the resensualization of the body and spirit than others. Many have been built within urban areas, or have been encircled and closed in by cities, and have lost a significant part of their special attraction. I suggest that you select inns located in the mountains or high above the ocean (as in Atami), as far removed from the world of high technology as possible.

Technology is not sexy. Instead of appealing to the sensual side of a person (which our civilization misunderstands, misuses, and abuses) advanced industrial systems actually arouse certain primordial fears that are linked with loss of freedom and a sterile rather than the richly emotional existence so important to the human psyche. In fact, in recent years, behavioral scientists have become aware of a direct relationship between sexual maladjustment and so-called progress based on technology. Progress, in the current sense of the word, induces depression, which in turn produces sexual inadequacies. A few nights in a ryokan helps to relieve this depression and restore interest in the sensual side of life.

The traditional culture of Japan was erotic in principle, and it is this sensual orientation in Japanese inns that gave them a special role in Japanese history—a role they continue to play today to those who understand and take advantage of them.

Any visitor who comes to Japan on vacation and fails to spend a few days in a traditional Japanese ryokan is missing much of the point of the trip.

Chapter VII

Nihongo
A Little Language
Goes a Long Way

You *Can* Speak Japanese

Quite frankly, Japanese is a very difficult language to master unless you learn it naturally as a child. The reason for this difficulty is that there are several forms and levels of Japanese that are normally used in different situations, which are determined by the relative ages of the speaker and speakee, by their sex, by their social status, their business rank, whether it is a formal or informal occasion, whether the two are friends from their school years or afterward, and so on. There are at least half a dozen other situations that affect how the language is used.

All of the above has to do with the language in its spoken form. There are also several other distinct forms that are appropriate for formal speeches, for broadcasting the news on radio or television, and for writing the news in newspapers or magazines.

Of course, the newcomer to the language can simply forget about most of the above situations or forms of the language because he or she is not going to start broadcasting news, make speeches, or be called on to respond in formal high-toned Japanese.

And, fortunately, there is one standard conversational form that is much easier to learn, including its polite form, and it is perfectly acceptable to the Japanese when used by anyone who speaks only a little of the language and is still in the early stages of learning.

In fact, this conversational form of Japanese (which has been called "mother's Japanese") is especially easy for English speakers to learn because the pronunciation is very similar to Spanish, and the grammatical structure of the language is such that you can communicate a broad range of concepts and ideas with a vocabulary of just a hundred or so words.

For example, the English sentence "I want to eat" is a rather complex grammatical structure with a subject, verb, and object. In Japanese you can express exactly the same thought or meaning with one word: *tabetai* (tah-bay-tie). If you want to say, "I don't want to eat," all you have to do is use the negative form of the verb meaning "to eat," i.e. *tabetakunai* (tah-bay-tah-kuu-nie).

This is true for literally hundreds of other thoughts. Another example: "I want to go"—*Ikitai* (ee-kee-tie). And the negative: "I don't want to go"—*Ikitakunai* (ee-kee-tah-kuu-nie).

The past and future tenses of these words are just as simple and in ordinary usage are the equivalent of saying a full sentence: "I ate (already)"—*Tabemashita* (tah-bay-mahssh-tah). "I will eat"—*Tabemasu* (tah-bay-mahss).

By memorizing or just reading the present, past, negative, and desiderative form of a hundred different words, you can express four hundred complete thoughts. That is enough to get you in or out of a lot of trouble. Add another hundred nouns, pronouns, adjectives, and adverbs to the above and you can qualify as a genuine linguist to your envious friends.

Japanese Made Easy

The Japanese language is made up of syllables based on only six sounds: a (ah), i (ee), u (ou / not yuu), e (eh), o (oh), and n (like the *n* in *bond*). The following pronunciation charts include all the sounds and syllables in the Japanese language, with their English-language phonetic equivalents. To pronounce the syllables correctly, all you have to do is read the phonetic sounds in English.

Japanese Pronunciation Chart #1
(In Japanese and Phonetically)

A	I	U	E	O
ah	ee	uu	eh	oh
KA	**KI**	**KU**	**KE**	**KO**
kah	kee	kuu	kay	koe
SA	**SHI**	**SU**	**SE**	**SO**
sah	she	sue	say	soe
TA	**CHI**	**TSU**	**TE**	**TO**
tah	chee	t'sue	tay	toe
NA	**NI**	**NU**	**NE**	**NO**
nah	nee	nuu	nay	no
HA	**HI**	**HU**	**HE**	**HO**
hah	he	who	hay	hoe
MA	**MI**	**MU**	**ME**	**MO**
mah	me	moo	may	moe

Japanese Pronunciation Chart #1 (Continued)
(In Japanese and Phonetically)

YA	I	U	E	YO
yah	ee	uu	eh	yoe
RA	**RI**	**RU**	**RE**	**RO**
rah	ree	rue	ray	roe

(Trill the *R's* a bit if you can)

GA	GI	GU	GE	GO
gah	gee	goo	gay	go

(As in "geese")

ZA	JI	ZU	ZE	ZO
zah	jee	zoo	zay	zoe
DA	**JI**	**ZU**	**DE**	**DO**
dah	jee	zoo	day	doe
BA	**BI**	**BU**	**BE**	**BO**
bah	bee	boo	bay	boe
PA	**PI**	**PU**	**PE**	**PO**
pah	pee	puu	pay	poe

Pronunciation Chart #2
(The following 33 syllables are combinations of some of those appearing above. Pronounce the two-part phonetic aids rather rapidly, "binding" the parts together. Pronounce other combinations as one syllable.)

RYA	RYU	RYO
re-yah	re-yuu	re-yoe

(Trill the *R's* a bit)

MYA	MYU	MYO
me-yah	me-yuu	me-yoe

NYA	**NYU**	**NYO**
ne-yah	ne-yuu	ne-yoe
HYA	**HYU**	**HYO**
he-yah	he-yuu	he-yoe
CHA	**CHU**	**CHO**
chah	chuu	choe
SHA	**SHU**	**SHO**
shah	shuu	show
KYA	**KYU**	**KYO**
q'yah	que	q-yoe
PYA	**PYU**	**PYO**
p'yah	p'yuu	p'yoe
BYA	**BYU**	**BYO**
b'yah	b'yuu	b'yoe
JA	**JU**	**JO**
jah	juu	joe
GYA	**GYU**	**GYO**
g'yah	g'yuu	g'yoe

Japanese You Can Use

Tabemasu *(tah-bay-mahss)*
I eat.
I will eat (now).
I do eat (it *or* that).

Tabetai *(tah-bay-tie)*
I want to eat.

Tabetakunai *(tah-bay-tah-kuu-nie)*
I don't want to eat.

Tabemashita *(tah-bay-mahssh-tah)*
I ate (already).
He, she, it ate.

Tabemasen *(tah-bay-mah-sin)*
I do not eat (that).
I'm not going to eat.
I did not eat *(if asked)*.

Tabemasen deshita *(ta-bay-mah-sin desh-tah)*
I did not eat.

Tabemasho *(tah-bay-mah-show)*
Let's eat.

Tabete kudasai *(tah-bay-tay kuu-dah-sie)*
Please eat (it *or* now).

Tabemasu ka? *(tah-bay-mahss kah?)*
Are you going to eat?
Do you eat (it, that)?

Tabetai desu ka? *(tah-bay-tie dess kah?)*
Do you want to eat?

Nomimasu *(no-me-mahss)*
I drink.
I will drink (now).
I do drink (it *or* that).

Nomitai *(no-me-tie)*
I want to drink.

Nomitakunai *(no-me-tah-kuu-nie)*
I don't want to drink (now *or* it).

Nomimashita *(no-me-mahssh-tah)*
I drank (already).
He, she, it drank.

Nomimasen *(no-me-mah-sin)*
I do not drink.
I'm not going to drink.
I did not drink yet *(if asked)*.
He, she does not drink.

Nomimasen deshita *(no-me-mah-sin desh-tah)*
I did not drink.

Nomimasho *(no-me-mah-show)*
Let's drink.

Nonde kudasai *(noan-day kuu-dah-sie)*
Please drink (it *or* now).

Nomimasu ka? *(no-me-mahss kah?)*
Do you drink (that)?
Will you drink (something)?

Nomitai desu ka? *(no-me-tie dess kah?)*
Do you want to drink (something)?

Ikimasu *(ee-kee-mahss)*
I go.
I am going.
I will go.

Ikitai *(ee-kee-tie)*
I want to go.

Ikitakunai *(ee-kee-tah-kuu-nie)*
I don't want to go.

Ikimashita *(ee-kee-mahssh-tah)*
I went.
He, she, it went.

Ikimasen *(ee-kee-mah-sin)*
I do not go.
I am not going.
I did not go *(if asked)*.

Ikimasen deshita *(ee-kee-mah-sin desh-tah)*
I did not go.

Ikimasho *(ee-kee-mah-show)*
Let's go.

Itte kudasai *(eat-tay kuu-dah-sie)*
Please go.

Ikimasu ka? *(ee-kee-mahss kah?)*
Are you going?
Is he, she going?

Ikitai desu ka? *(ee-kee-tie dess kah?)*
Do you want to go?

Moraimasu *(moe-rye-mahss)*
I will receive (it).
I will accept (it).

Moraitai *(moe-rye-tie)*
I want to receive (take) it.

Moraitakunai *(moe-rye-tah-kuu-nie)*
I don't want to receive (accept) it.

Moraimashita *(moe-rye-mahssh-tah)*
I received it.

Moraimasen *(moe-rye-mah-sin)*
I didn't receive it.

Moraimasen deshita *(moe-rye-mah-sin desh-tah)*
I did not receive it.

Moraimasho *(moe-rye-mah-show)*
I'll receive (take) it.
Let's receive (take) it.

Moratte kudasai *(moe-rot-tay kuu-dah-sie)*
Please receive (take) it.

Moraimasu ka? *(moe-rye-mahss kah?)*
Will you take (receive) it?

Moraitai desu ka? *(moe-rye-tie dess kah?)*
Would you like to receive/take it?

Kaimasu *(kie-mahss)*
I will buy (it).

Kaitai *(kie-tai)*
I want to buy (it/that).

Kaitakunai *(kie-tah-kuu-nie)*
I don't want to buy it/that.

Kaimashita *(kie-mahssh-tah)*
I bought it.
He, she bought it.

Kaimasen *(kie-mah-sin)*
I'm not going to buy it.
I didn't buy it *(if asked)*.

Kaimasen deshita *(kie-mah-sin desh-tah)*
I did not buy (it).

Kaimasho *(kie-mah-show)*
I'll buy it.
Let's buy it.

Katte kudasai *(kot-tay kuu-dah-sie)*
Please buy it.

Kaimasu ka? *(kie-mahss kah?)*
Are you going to buy it?

Kaitai desu ka? *(kie-tie dess kah?)*
Would you like to buy it?

Kikimasu *(kee-kee-mahss)*
I hear.
I can hear *(if asked)*.

Kikitai *(kee-kee-tie)*
I want to hear.

Kikitakunai *(kee-kee-tah-kuu-nie)*
I don't want to hear.

Kikimashita *(kee-kee-mahssh-tah)*
I heard (it).

Kikimasen *(kee-kee-mah-sin)*
I don't hear it.
I didn't hear it *(if asked)*.

Kikimasen deshita *(kee-kee-mah-sin desh-tah)*
I did not hear (it).

Kikimasho *(kee-kee-mah-show)*
Let's listen?

Kiite kudasai *(keet-tay kuu-dah-sie)*
Please listen.

Kikimasu ka? *(kee-kee-mahss kah?)*
Are you going to listen?

Kikitai desu ka? *(kee-kee-tie dess kah?)*
Would you like to hear?

Kimasu *(kee-mahss)*
I am coming.

Kitai *(kee-tai)*
I want to come.

Kitakunai *(kee-tah-kuu-nie)*
I don't want to come.

Kimashita *(kee-mahssh-tah)*
I came.
He, she, it came.

Kimasen *(kee-mah-sin)*
I am not coming.
He, she, it is not coming.

Kimasen deshita *(kee-mah-sin desh-tah)*
I, he, she did not come.

Kimasho *(kee-mah-show)*
Let's come.

Kimasu ka? *(kee-mahss kah?)*
Are you, he, she coming?

Kitai desu ka? *(kee-tie dess kah?)*
Do you want to come?
Does she, he want to come?

Mimasu *(me-mahss)*
I see.
I will see.

Mitai *(me-tie)*
I want to see (it, that).

Mitakunai *(mee-tah-kuu-nie)*
I don't want to see (it, that).

Mimashita *(me-mahssh-tah)*
I saw (it, him, her).

Mimasen *(me-mah-sin)*
I don't see (it).

Mimasen deshita *(me-mah-sin desh-tah)*
I didn't see (it).

Mimasho *(me-mah-show)*
Let's see (it).

Mite kudasai *(me-tay kuu-dah-sie)*
Please look (at it).

Mimasu ka? *(me-mahss kah?)*
Do you see (it)?
Will you see (it)?

Mitai desu ka? *(me-tie dess kah?)*
Do you want to see it?

Yomimasu *(yoe-me-mahss)*
I read (it).

Yomitai *(yoe-me-tie)*
I want to read.
I want to read it.

Yomitakunai *(yoe-me-tah-kuu-nie)*
I don't want to read.
I don't want to read it.

Yomimashita *(yoe-me-mahssh-tah)*
I read it.

Yomimasen *(yoe-me-mah-sin)*
I do not read.

Yomimasen deshita *(yoe-me-mah-sin desh-tah)*
I did not read (it).

Yomimasho *(yoe-mah-show)*
Let's read.

Yonde kudasai *(yoan-day kuu-dah-sie)*
Please read.
Please read it.

Yomimasu ka? *(yoe-me-mahss kah?)*
Are you going to read it?

Yomitai desu ka? *(yoe-me-tie dess kah?)*
Would you like to read (it)?

Arimasu *(ah-ree-mahss)*
There is (something exists; I have something).

Arimashita *(ah-ree-mahssh-tah)*
There was (I had something; it was there).

Arimasu ka? *(ah-ree-mahss kah?)*
Do you have some?
Do you have it?
Are there any?

Arimasen *(ah-ree-mah-sin)*
I don't have it.
There isn't any.

Arimashita ka? *(ah-ree-mahssh-tah kah?)*
Did you have it?
Was there any?

Kakimasu *(kah-kee-mahss)*
I write.
I will write.

Kakitai *(kah-kee-tie)*
I want to write.

Kakitakunai *(kah-kee-tah-kuu-nie)*
I don't want to write.

Kakimashita *(kah-kee-mahssh-tah)*
I, he, she wrote.

Kakimasen *(kah-kee-mah-sin)*
I, he, she do not write.

Kakimasen deshita *(kah-kee-mah-sin desh-tah)*
I, he, she did not write.

Kakimasho *(kah-kee-mah-show)*
Let's write.

Kaite kudasai *(kite-tay kuu-dah-sie)*
Please write.

Kikimasu ka? *(kah-kee-mahss kah?)*
Do you write?
Will you write?

Kakitai desu ka? *(kah-kee-tie dess kah?)*
Do you want to write?

Haraimasu *(hah-rye-mahss)*
I will pay.

Haraitai *(hah-rye-tie)*
I want to pay.

Haraitakunai *(hah-rye-tah-kuu-nie)*
I don't want to pay.

Haraimashita *(hah-rye-mahssh-tah)*
I paid.

Haraimasen *(hah-rye-mah-sin)*
I do not pay.
I will not pay.

Haraimasen deshita *(hah-rye-mah-sin desh-tah)*
I did not pay.

Haraimasho *(hah-rye-mah-show)*
Let's pay.

Haratte kudasai *(hah-rot-tay kuu-dah-sie)*
Please pay.

Haraimasu ka? *(hah-rye-mahss kah?)*
Are you going to pay?
Will you pay?

Haraitai desu ka? *(hah-rye-tie dess kah?)*
Would you like to pay?

Yarimasu *(yah-ree-mahss)*
I will do it.

Yaritai *(yah-ree-tie)*
I want to do it.

Yaritakunai *(yah-ree-tah-kuu-nie)*
I don't want to do it.

Yarimashita *(yah-ree-mahssh-tah)*
I did it.

Yarimasen *(yah-ree-mah-sin)*
I do not do it.

Yarimasen deshita *(yah-ree-mah-sin desh-tah)*
I did not do it.

Yarimasho *(yah-ree-mah-show)*
Let's do it.

Yatte kudasai *(yaht-tay kuu-dah-sie)*
Please do it.

Yarimasu ka? *(yah-ree-mahss kah?)*
Will you do it?

Yaritai desu ka? *(yah-ree-tie dess kah?)*
Would you like to do it?

Kaerimasu *(kie-ree-mahss)*
I will return.
He, she will return.

Kaeritai *(kie-ree-tie)*
I want to return.

Kaeritakunai *(kie-ree-tah-kuu-nie)*
I don't want to return.

Kaerimashita *(kie-ree-mahssh-tah)*
I returned.
He, she returned.

Kaerimasen *(kie-ree-mah-sin)*
I will not return.
He, she will not return.

Kaerimasen deshita *(kie-ree-mah-sin desh-tah)*
I did not return.
He, she did not return.

Kaerimasho *(kie-ree-mah-show)*
Let's return.

Kaette kudasai *(kite-tay kuu-dah-sie)*
Please return.

Kaerimasu ka? *(kie-ree-mahss kah?)*
Will you return?
Will he, she return?

Kaeritai desu ka? *(kie-ree-tie dess kah?)*
Do you want to return?

Personal Pronouns

Personal pronouns *(I, we, you, he, she, they)* are not used as often in Japanese as they are in English. Well over half of the time, the appropriate pronoun is "understood" because the meaning is more or less built into the verb used, or it is understood from the context of the sentence—as demonstrated by the single-word "sentences" above.

There are, however, many occasions when it is not only proper but necessary to use the personal pronouns. Here they are:

I	**watakushi**	*(wah-tock-she)*
we	**watakushi-tachi**	*(wah-tock-she-tah-chee)*
you	(singular) **anata**	*(ah-nah-tah)*
you	(plural) **anata-tachi**	*(ah-nah-tah-tah-chee)*

he   **anohito** *(ah-no-ssh-toe)*
she   **kanojo** *(kah-no-joe)*
they **anohitotachi** *(ah-no-ssh-toe-tah-chee)*
There are some other forms of several of these words, but they are not necessary for basic communication, and can be ignored for the time being.

How to Use Numbers

Numbers are one of the most important foundations for communicating. In Japanese there are two numbering systems from one through ten, but only one system from eleven on. The first system, which is only for one through ten, is native Japanese, while the other complete system is imported from China. The first system is used for counting some things but not others. The same goes for the second system when the things to be counted are one through ten.
Here is the first system:

one   **hitotsu** *(he-tote-sue)*
two   **futatsu** *(fuu-tot-sue)*
three **mittsu** *(meet-sue)*
four   **yottsu** *(yote-sue)*
five   **itsutsu** *(eet-sue-t'sue)*
six   **muttsu** *(moot-sue)*
seven **nanatsu, nana** *(nah-not-sue, nah-nah)*
eight **yattsu** *(yaht-sue)*
nine   **kokonotsu** *(koe-koe-note-sue)*
ten   **to** *(toe)*

When counting things (1 through 10) that, like hamburgers, are not specifically flat or cylindrical, the above system is used—*hambaaga futatsu* (two hamburgers); *donatsu muttsu* (six donuts), etc.
When denoting "one person" and "two persons," *hitotsu* and *futatsu* are combined with a compound that means

"person": *hitori* (one person); *futari* (two persons). From three on, the Chinese system is used. Here is the Chinese system:

one	**ichi** *(e-chee)*
two	**ni** *(nee)*
three	**san** *(sahn)*
four	**shi** *(she)*, Yon *(yoan)*
five	**go** *(go)*
six	**roku** *(roe-kuu)*
seven	**shichi** *(she-chee)*
eight	**hachi** *(hah-chee)*
nine	**ku** *(kuu)*
ten	**ju** *(juu)*

From 11 to 99, all you do is combine the numbers above: 11 is ten plus one or *ju-ichi;* 12 is ten plus two or *ju-ni;* 19 is ten plus nine or *ju-ku.* Twenty is made up of two tens: *ni-ju;* 21 is *ni-ju-ichi;* 22 is *ni-ju-ni,* and so on to thirty, which is three tens or *san-ju.* Forty is *yon-ju;* fifty is *go-ju;* and so on. Ninety-nine is *kyu-ju-kyu* (nine tens plus nine). The spelling change from *ku* to *kyu* (que) is done for ease in pronunciation.

The word for 100 is *hyaku* (he-yah-kuu). From 100 to 199 follows exactly the same pattern as above: 101 is *hyaku-ichi;* 102 is *hyaku-ni;* 150 is *hayku-go-ju;* and so on to 199, which is *hyaku-kyu-ju-kyu.* Two hundred is *ni-hyaku,* which also follows suit (*Ni-hyaku-ichi, ni-hyaku-ni,* etc.).

The rest of the hundreds are: *sambyaku* (sahm-be-yah-kuu), *yon-hyaku* (yoan-he-yah-kuu); *go-hyaku* (go-he-yah-kuu); *roppyaku* (rope-p'yah-kuu—note euphonic change); *nana-hyaku* (nah-nah-he-yah-kuu); *happyaku* (hop-p'yah-kuu); *kyu-hyaku* (que-he-rah-kuu).

There is another word for "thousand": *sen* (sin). Once again, 1,001, 1,002, etc., are combinations of the word for thousand plus the other appropriate numbers: 1,050 = *sen-go-ju;* 1,260 = *sen-ni-hyaku-roku-ju;* 1,500 is *sen-go-hyaku.* Two thousand is *ni-sen;* 3,000 is *san-sen* (which is changed to *san-zen* for clarity in pronunciation).

This system goes up to 10,000, for which there is again a special word: *man* (mahn). Ten thousand is *ichi-man;* 10,500 is *ichi-man-go-hyaku;* 20,000 is of course *ni-man;* 50,000 is *go-man,* and so on up to one million, which is 100 *man* or *hyaku-man;* 2,000,000 is *ni-hyaku-man;* 5,000,000 is *go-hyaku-man,* etc. Ten million is *ichi-oku* (e-chee-oh-kuu).

Ordinal Numbers

To change the cardinal numbers to ordinal, just add *bamme* (bahm-may) to each of the numbers: 1st = *ichi-bamme;* 2nd = *ni-bamme;* 10th = *ju-bamme;* 21st = *ni-ju-ichi-bamme.*

Counting Other Things

There is a special class of words in Japanese (called numeratives in English) that are used when counting specific things like people, animals, flat things, round things, birds, cups or glasses of liquids, books, etc. Altogether there are about thirty of these class-words, but the most common half dozen will get you in and out of Japan with style. They are:

Nin *(neen),* for person or people: five people = *go-nin;* ten people = *ju-nin.*

Hiki *(he-kee),* for animals, fish, and insects (with euphonic changes): one animal = *ippiki* (eep-pee-kee); five animals = *go-hiki.*

Wa *(wah),* used to count birds—*ichi-wa; ni-wa; sam-ba* (euphonic change); *shi-wa.*

Satsu *(sot-sue),* used for counting books or magazines: *is-satsu; ni-satsu; go-satsu; ju-satsu.*

Hon *(hoan)*, used for counting long, round things, like pencils, fingers, rope, poles, etc.: *ippon; ni-hon; sam-bon* (euphonic change); *yon-hon; go-hon; juppon* (jupe-poan).

Mai *(my)*, for counting flat things, like paper, sheets, boards, trays, etc., i.e. *ichi-mai; ni-mai; san-mai; hachi-mai; ju-mai.*

Hai *(hie)*, for counting cups or glasses of liquids: *ippai; ni-hai; sam-bai* (euphonic change); *yon-hai; ku-hai; jippai* (jeep-pie).

How to Tell Time

Time, in the sense of "what time is it?" is expressed in Japanese by the word *ji* (jee). "What" is *nani* (nah-nee) or in this case, *nan* (nahn). So: "What time is it?" = *Nan ji desu ka?* (nahn jee dess kah?).

Here is the time system:

1 o'clock   **ichi ji** *(ee-chee jee)*
2 o'clock   **ni ji** *(nee jee)*
3 o'clock   **san ji** *(sahn jee)*, etc. Just add *ji* to the proper number.

Han (hahn) is the word for "half," so 6:30 is *roku ji han;* 12:30 is of course *ju-ni ji han.*

To say "It is 3:30," just say *san ji han desu* (sahn jee hahn dess).

The Days of the Week

You cannot get very far in life these days without knowing the days of the week. This is especially important while traveling. The days of the week in Japanese are:

Monday   **getsuyobi** *(gate-sue-yoe-bee)*
Tuesday   **kayobi** *(kah-yoe-bee)*

Wednesday	**suiyobi** *(sooey-yoe-bee)*
Thursday	**mokuyobi** *(moke-yoe-bee)*
Friday	**kinyobi** *(keen-yoe-bee)*
Saturday	**doyobi** *(doe-yoe-bee)*
Sunday	**nichiyobi** *(nee-chee-yoe-bee)*

Periods of the Day/Week

today	**kyo** (k'yoe)
tonight	**komban** (kome-bahn)
tomorrow	**ashita** (ahssh-tah)
day after tomorrow	**assatte** (ah-sot-tay)
tomorrow morning	**ashita-no asa** (ahssh-tah-no ah-sah)
tomorrow night	**ashita-no ban** (ahssh-tah-no bahn)
yesterday	**kino** (kee-no)
last night	**yube** (yuu-bay)
day before yesterday	**ototoi** (oh-toe-toy)
morning	**asa** (ah-sah)
this morning	**kesa** (kay-sah)
this afternoon	**kyo gogo** (k'yoe go-go)

The Months

January	**ichigatsu** (ee-chee-got-sue)
February	**nigatsu** (nee-got-sue)
March	**sangatsu** (sahn-got-sue)
April	**shigatsu** (she-got-sue)
May	**gogatsu** (go-got-sue)
June	**rokugatsu** (roe-kuu-got-sue)
July	**shichigatsu** (she-chee-got-sue)
August	**hachigatsu** (hah-chee-got-sue)
September	**kugatsu** (kuu-got-sue)
October	**jugatsu** (juu-got-sue)
November	**juichigatsu** (juu-ee-chee-got-sue)
December	**junigatsu** (juu-nee-got-sue)

Other important words that you can use to get across relatively complex thoughts:

Good morning	**Ohaiyo goazaimasu** *(oh-hie-yoe go-zie-mahss)*
Good afternoon	**Konnichi wa** *(koan-nee-chee wah)*
Good evening	**Komban wa** *(koam-bahn wah)*
Thank you very much	**Arigato gozaimasu** *(ah-ree-gah-toe go-zie-mahss)*
Excuse me	**Sumimasen** *(sue-me-mah-sin)*
When?	**Itsu?** *(eet-sue)*
Where?	**Doko?** *(doe-koe)*
What?	**Nani?** *(nah-nee)*
Mine	**Wataskushi-no** *(wah-tock-she-no)*
Yours	**Anato-no** *(ah-nah-tah-no)*
Enough	**Jubun** *(juu-boon)*
Expensive	**Takai** *(tah-kie)*
Cheap	**Yasui** *(yah-sue-ee)*
Big	**Okii** *(oh-kee)*
Small	**Chiisai** *(chee-sie)*
Delicious	**Oishii** *(oh-ee-shee)*
Hot	**Atsui** *(aht-sue-ee)*
Cold	**Samui** *(sah-muu-ee)*
Warm	**Atatakai** *(ah-tah-tah-kie)*
Hurry!	**Hayaku!** *(hah-yah-kuu)*
Slowly	**Yukkuri** *(yuke-kuu-ree)*
Goodby	**Sayonara** *(sah-yoe-nah-rah)*

You can see from the foregoing that learning how to use a great deal of Japanese is not a major undertaking. If you would like to considerably expand your choice of words and sentences, I recommend my *Japanese in Plain English* (Passport Books), which contains some 1,200 of the most common words in the Japanese language, with example sentences (all phoneticized) for practical daily use.

CHAPTER VIII

Gochiso-Sama!
Pleasuring the Palate

Overcoming Gastrophobia

The travel industry discovered a long time ago that the most important thing in whether or not people enjoy themselves when they are away from home is how well they eat. People will put up with almost anything if the food is really outstanding. This particularly applies to traveling abroad, because visitors are regularly subjected to new and unusual experiences that are often upsetting.

When we are home eating our familiar diet, we spend very little time thinking about the psychology of food or how it affects us physiologically. But when we are asked to eat food we are not familiar with, everything changes. We are immediately interested in the ingredients, what it looks like, how it smells, and finally how it tastes—and this is when our cultural conditioning, especially our biases, really shows. If it is our first experience with a particular cuisine, we also soon discover that some unfamiliar foods have an immediate and sometimes serious physical effect on our bodies.

I began eating a Japanese diet on a daily basis in the early

1950s, when I was a student in Tokyo, because I couldn't afford meat dishes or other dishes that were similar to the American food I had been raised on. Subsisting primarily on rice and noodles, I almost always felt hungry (and produced a lot more gas than usual). I do not recommend that visitors go this far.

I also recall that when the Japanese first started traveling abroad in the early post-war period, the majority of them would be ill by about the third day from eating meals with lots of meat and butter. In some cases, the illness was so severe they returned to Japan before finishing their trip.

But visitors to Japan today need have no reservations or fears about being able to eat a diet that is compatible with their system and pleasing to their palate. Japanese cuisine has come a long way since the early 1950s—not that all of what is now available in Japan is necessarily the healthiest kind of food to eat, but there are dozens of meat, seafood, poultry, and vegetable dishes that are outstanding gastronomic experiences, and will not make you ill or leave you feeling famished.

Again, the primary factor is not a lack of good food but reluctance on the part of many visitors to try dishes that look and sound unfamiliar. Many first-time visitors to Japan allow their conditioned responses to control them in what they eat. And I'm not talking about raw fish or dried octopus or any of the other uncooked or uncommon foods that are considered gourmet treats by the Japanese but evoke responses that range from caution to disgust among many Westerners.

There are, in fact, a few Japanese foods that one generally has to grow up with to be able to eat with any degree of satisfaction, much less develop a taste for. These include (for me, anyway) uncooked *mochi* (moe-chee), *natto* (nottoe, and a couple of varieties of sea slugs.

Mochi is a glutinous mass made from cooked rice that

has been kneaded and pounded until it has the consistency and taste of a very heavy paste. I don't mind it at all when it is fried, but raw or boiled is another matter. Natto is fermented beans, which, as the Japanese readily admit, look bad, smell bad, and taste bad. But it is a traditional dish that is highly regarded by most older Japanese (the younger set often prefers cowboy beans or French fries).

In addition to dozens of dishes that might be described as Japanized versions of popular Western foods, there are an equal number of dishes that are traditional, or have been developed over the past several decades, that are pleasing to most palates at first taste. Some of these are dishes of true gourmet quality that would not be out of place in the finest restaurants in the U.S. or Europe.

The Best Dishes of Japan

The following list of Japanese dishes are ones that I regularly recommend to foreign friends and guests visiting Japan, and which have proven to be the most acceptable to the majority of people over a period of many years:

Mizu-taki *(me-zoo-tah-kee)*—A recent informal survey found that mizu-taki was the most popular wintertime dish in Japan. It consists of small pieces of chicken, leeks, Chinese cabbage, vermicelli, and tofu boiled in an earthen pot containing a stock made from water and dried fish-shavings. Other vegetables may be added to taste. Each piece is dipped in a spicy sauce before eating.

Suki-yaki *(sue-kee-yah-kee)*—People who like meat generally love suki-yaki. It consists of thin slices of beef boiled in a slightly sweetened shoyu-sake stock with mushrooms, leeks, Chinese cabbage, vermicelli, and chunks of tofu. Aficionados dip the meat (and the other ingredients as well) into a stirred raw egg dip before eating—with rice.

Nabe-mono *(nah-bay moe-no)*—Literally "earthenware pot things," nabe-mono refers to a number of popular hot-pot dishes made up of different ingredients. *Chiri nabe* (chee-ree nah-bay) consists of fish (usually cod) boiled with cabbage, leeks, carrot slices, mushrooms, and tofu, dipped in a spicy sauce before eating. *Dote nabe* (doe-tay nah-bay) is made up of oysters, leeks, tofu, edible chrysanthemum leaves, and chunks of carrot in a casserole that includes sweetened miso paste. A raw egg is usually served as a dip. Another nabe-mono version, *yose nabe,* (yoe-say nah-bay) has both chicken and fish as its main ingredient.

Tempura *(tim-puu-rah)*—One of the most popular of all Japanese dishes, tempura consists of selected seafoods and vegetables coated in a special batter and deep-fried. Among the items most commonly found in tempura: shrimp or prawns, whitefish, eggplant, green peppers, onions, a slice of sweet potato, string beans, a square of nori, and beefsteak plant. A light, delicate dip, in which each piece is dipped before eating, is served on the side. Seasoned tempura eaters mix a bit of grated horseradish into the dip before using. Tempura is served with a bowl of rice, soup, and small chunks of pickles.

Tonkatsu *(tone-kot-sue)*—A pork filet or roast steak breaded in a flour-egg batter and deep-fried, tonkatsu is a typical Japanese dish that most visitors thoroughly enjoy the first time they try it. It is served with shredded cabbage (and in some restaurants, potato salad), soup, and rice. Experienced gourmets put a kind of steak sauce on their tonkatsu, and shoyu on the shredded cabbage.

Okonomi-yaki *(oh-koe-no-me-yah-kee)*—This is the quiche of Japan. It is a pancake (thick or thin, depending on the style of the vendor or restaurant) made from a batter containing chopped vegetables, meats, seafoods, and eggs. Street-stand vendors usually have only one thin version. In specialty restaurants, you can usually specify if you want beef, chicken, or seafood as the main ingredient. The more expensive thick versions can be a full meal.

Shabu Shabu *(shah-buu shah-buu)*—Another dish that is cooked on the diners' table, shabu shabu is thin slices of very tender beef, leeks, Chinese cabbage, and tofu boiled in a large copper or brass pot (with a chimney) filled with water or stock. The meat takes only seconds to cook. Before eating, each piece or bite is dipped in a sauce made of miso, sesame seeds, and shoyu, or in a second dip made of lemon juice and grated radish.

Teppan-yaki *(tape-pahn-yah-kee)*—This is the style of grill-cooking made famous in the U.S. by the Benihana restaurant chain. In the more expensive places that cater to visitors, guests are seated around large grills attended by individual chefs. A selection of vegetables that usually includes onions, green peppers, bean sprouts, and mushrooms, along with chunks of beef or pork, are grilled to the guests' specifications. In less expensive places, the grills are built into tables (often booth-style), and the guests do their own cooking. Many teppan-yaki houses grill the meat in chopped-up garlic and oil.

Udon Suki *(uu-doan ski)*—Another hot dish that is a favorite in winter, udon suki includes chunks of chicken and sometimes shrimp or clams, leeks, mushrooms, chrysanthemum leaves, and white noodles boiled in a suki-yaki sauce.

Sushi *(sue-she)*—Almost everyone knows by this time that sushi is slices of raw fish and other seafood nestled on buns of lightly vinegared and sweetened rice. There are over a dozen commonly used sushi fish, along with clams, abalone, fish eggs, sea chestnut eggs, octopus, squid, and conger eel. If you are not already a sushi fan, it might be best to start out with tuna *(maguro),* since it does not have a fishy taste and is not tough or stringy. You can order the different kinds of sushi one at a time (just by pointing to them if you are at a sushi bar) to discover which ones you like best. Many shops place a small dab of greenish horse-radish *(wasabi* / wah-sah-bee) under the slab of seafood on some of their sushi. It is very hot and you may want to remove it or leave only a bit of it. If you don't want it there in the first place, just say *Sabi nuki* (sah-bee nuu-kee), which means "without horseradish."

Oyako Donburi *(oh-yah-koe doan-buu-ree)*—This is a bowl of rice covered with pieces of chicken and onions cooked in egg. It is a very simple and inexpensive dish that is available in most soba and udon noodle shops as well as general *(shokudo* / show-kuu-doe) restaurants. Unless the restaurant is really below par, the dish usually ranges from tasty to delicious, and it is filling.

There are dozens of other rice dishes, including many with toppings such as curry, beef-stew gravy, suki-yaki type meat, or tempura-style shrimp, along with several versions of fried rice (with chopped up vegetables, meats, chicken, shrimp or crab, and egg), plus the same or similar rice mixtures boiled together in a pot, and called *kama-meshi* (kah-mah-may-she) or "pot food," but generally speaking, one has to acquire a taste for these dishes, primarily be-cause the main ingredient is rice.

Yaki-tori—This worldwide favorite is nothing more than small chunks of chicken (and liver, if you want), green peppers, and onions (or leeks) on bamboo or metal skew-ers, grilled over charcoal. Just before serving, or during the process of grilling, they are salted or dipped into a shoyu-based barbecue sauce, depending on your choice. Yakitori is usually eaten as a snack rather than a full meal, especially when eaten at outside sidewalk vendors. In restaurants, a yaki-tori meal would include rice, soup, and probably pickles.

Adventures in Good Eating

There are dozens of well-known restaurants in Tokyo, Kyoto, Osaka, Kobe, and other large Japanese cities that are famous as specialty restaurants, noted for their steaks, crab-meat dishes, tempura, sushi, tofu dishes, teppan-yaki, baked eel, pot-boiled "stews," and so on, plus such ethnic restaurants as Chinese, French, German, Greek, Indian, Italian, Mexican, and Russian. These are the restaurants that advertise in English to the foreign community and to visitors from abroad, and generally range from good to excellent.

Many of these specialty restaurants, particularly the Japanese, are "experience places" with outstanding ethnic decor, and are an important part of the special pleasures of Japan. You won't have any trouble identifying or finding these places.

Eating Well for Less

If you are even a little bit adventurous—and want to economize on your food bills—you should also patronize the same restaurants as the average Japanese. These restaurants seldom if ever advertise and exist by the hundreds to the thousands in larger Japanese cities. They usually display plastic duplicates of the dishes they offer in showcases at the entrance. The duplicates are so realistic-looking that the uninitiated visitor to Japan often takes them for the real thing.

Both general and specialty restaurants utilize these plastic exhibits to advertise their wares, but to the foreign tourist they serve a second purpose as well. In addition to being graphic examples of the dishes available in individual restaurants, the dummy dishes are also a sign that the restaurant caters to the average local customer and is reasonably priced, since expensive restaurants, including restaurants that cater primarily to foreign residents and visitors, ordinarily do not display such plastic images.

Most general and specialty restaurants in Japan also have set breakfasts, lunches, and dinners, called *teishoku* (tay-e-show-kuu), that include a main course and side dishes. These set courses are invariably much cheaper than ordering a similar number of dishes à la carte (from one-half to two-thirds cheaper in many cases), so it is worthwhile to check them out. *Teishoku* meals are often displayed on trays (which is the way they are usually served).

General restaurants are known as *shokudo* (show-kuu-doe) or "places to eat" in Japanese, and are the Japanese equivalent of the typical American coffee shop, with breakfast, lunch, and dinner menus—the latter including several meat, chicken, and seafood dishes. While many of these dishes are prepared exactly the same way as in the U.S., the taste may differ somewhat because of the use of different condiments, and some of the side dishes may be a little different (an unfamiliar vegetable, for example). But you are getting a good, solid meal of meat, fish, or fowl with vegetables (and a dessert of ice cream, pie, cake, or fruit, if you like). In virtually all cases, you have a choice of a plate of rice or bread with the usual meal.

Shokudo are commonly found in department stores and office buildings; in, under, or near railway terminals, in shopping complexes, at airports, and along highways. (The coffee shops in Western-style hotels in Japan are *shokudo*, but they are usually quite a bit more expensive than outside restaurants and generally do not offer inexpensive set [*tei-shoku*] meals.)

Of course, you may eat solely in American-style fast-food restaurants while you are in major Japanese cities (McDonald's, Denny's, Wendy's, Anna Miller's, Victoria Station, etc.) at prices well below what one pays in hotel and "class" restaurants—but you should resort to these restaurants only in emergencies or to break a steady diet of unusual or exotic fare.

CHAPTER IX

Ofuro
When in Rome . . . !

The Traditions of Bathing

B athing regularly in hot water has been a solidly entrenched national custom in Japan since the beginning of recorded history. It probably dates back hundreds or even thousands of years earlier because bodily cleanliness is a paramount tenet of Shintoism, the native religion.

This practice alone was enough to distinguish the Japanese from the Chinese and Koreans and from most Westerners up until very recent times. When the first Westerners appeared in Japan, the Japanese could not stand to be near them very long because they smelled so.

Some foreigners, all of whom were men, who took up residence in Japan in the 1500s (before the government's exclusion policy) adapted rather quickly to the custom of regular bathing, not only because they discovered that it felt good to be clean and to not give off an offensive smell, but also because men and women bathed together, thus giving them a chance to see women in the nude.

But the first Western missionaries to reach Japan (the first one arrived in 1549) were shocked at the Japanese custom of bathing—first that they bathed regularly, and second, that they bathed together. Of course, it was the mixed-sex bathing that most upset the sex-obsessed missionaries, who saw the human body as an instrument of the devil, and themselves divinely charged to get the devil out of every damned soul they encountered.

Japanese converts to the Christian religion were prohibited from bathing more than once a week, while the missionaries themselves stayed as far away from water as possible (which could have been one of the reasons why they eventually failed to turn Japan into a Christianized nation—or at least I like to think so!).

Western missionaries were finally expelled from Japan just before the beginning of the 1600s because of their interference with internal political affairs and the threat that their activities would result in their home countries invading Japan—not because of their attitudes toward the Japanese custom of bathing.

Over two hundred and fifty years later, when missionaries were once again allowed to enter Japan, they very quickly demonstrated that they had not learned anything in the intervening centuries. They once again prohibited daily bathing and railed continuously against the Japanese custom of mixed-sex bathing.

Western missionaries still today have not succeeded in Christianizing Japan (and never will, of course), but their efforts did eventually play a major role in Japan's legally banning mixed-sex bathing in public bath facilities during the American military occupation of Japan.

I remember it as though it were yesterday. Bathhouses were given a grace period during which they were to build walls separating the baths into male and female sections. For several months prior to starting construction, many bathhouse operators strung a rope across the large common pool, with the portion on the left designated for men, and the right side for women.

Later, when the first solid partitions were put up, many of them separated only the washing area and the large soaking pool and about half of the undressing area. The operator on duty (who collected the small fee) was situated on a raised podium between the male and female sections. When you were standing beside the podium to pay your fee, you had a clear view of the female section of the bathhouse. It was not until years later that the two sections were completely separated in most bathhouses in the city areas.

With the coming of affluence in Japan and the construction of Western-style homes and apartments with built-in baths and showers, the number of public bathhouses dwindled. Well over half of the people in Japan now have their own private bathing facilities. Among my own circle of foreign friends who live in Japan, there are a few who still go to the local neighborhood bathhouse several times a week—daily, in fact, unless they have to work late. They follow the old custom because it adds a very special dimension to the routine of staying clean. It is a social experience, pleasing to both the mind and the body.

Mixed bathing in homes in Japan is still a common practice—although many of the tubs are so small they will accommodate only one person at a time. One of the nicest things about bathing with someone is that you have someone to scrub your back. What a wonderful feeling!

The Ritual of the Bath

The normal routine in a public bath or in a bath at a hot-spring spa is to carry any clean underclothing you intend to put on later with you to the bath, leave it and your *yukata* robe or other clothing in a plastic or wicker basket provided for that purpose in a dressing area outside of the bath proper, then enter the bath carrying your own soap and a *tenugui* (tay-nuu-gooey), a small combination washcloth and hand towel.

As you probably have heard by this time, you do not bathe in a Japanese bath. You scrub on the outside of the bath and then enter it to leasurely soak and chat with friends or fellow bathers. Washbasins, small buckets for ladling water out of the tub (or in larger places, hot and cold water spigots), along with low stools to sit on, are provided for bathers to douse themselves with hot water, scrub down, and rinse before climbing into the bath.

Bathing etiquette calls for both men and women to cover themselves discreetly with small hand towels when standing up and moving about in the bath. Women, of course, make no attempt to cover their breasts, since exposing them while bathing is not regarded as lewd or licentious in Japan.

Besides being much more sanitary and aesthetically pleasing to wash outside the tub you are going to soak in, mixed bathing provides many benefits that have been lost or downgraded in most Western societies. One of the greatest banes of Western civilizations is the hangup about human sexuality. There is a basic contradiction between the Western views of sexuality and reality, i.e., human needs, which results in friction, frustrations, and conflicts that have plagued our societies since cave days.

Mixed bathing does not solve all of these problems, but when done regularly from infancy by everyone it certainly eliminates many of the sources of sexual hangups, and reduces others. As a result of influence from the West, the Japanese custom of mixed bathing is unfortunately being eroded.

It is still common, however, to see scenes of mixed bathing regularly on national television, but again the scenes are invariably at hot-spring spas. On these televised programs both men and women cover their sex organs with small hand towels, so we are not talking about total frontal nudity on public TV. The TV scenes frequently show young bare-breasted women getting in and out of the pools, and sometimes exposing their breasts while they are in the water. But generally speaking, older women are not filmed unless their breasts are covered by a small towel or water. The rationale here is probably an arbitrary decision made by the TV people that the breasts of older women are not going to appeal to their audience.

Recently I watched a Sunday afternoon TV special on hot-spring spas in which the host was an attractive young woman. She was shown repeatedly in the nude, with only the little *tenugui* towel covering her pubic area, as she joined different groups of people, including men, in a variety of baths at different spas. In a number of cases, the only other bathers were men. She joined them with enviable savoire faire while carrying on a spritely commentary for the benefit of the viewing audience.

Now that is the kind of thing I would like to see on American television!

Taking the Plunge

I recall my own first experience in a mixed bath in Japan. It occurred in the latter part of the 1940s when I was a teen-aged member of the Occupation forces. The setting was a hot-springs spa in the foothills about two hours north of Tokyo. This, mind you, was shortly after the end of World War II when many Japanese in rural areas had never seen a Westerner in person, much less in the nude.

Just by luck, the bath that I chose to enter at that time

and in that place was fairly full—of females. There were three elderly women and about a dozen girls ranging in age from seventeen or eighteen down to five or six.

At that time, I understood only basic Japanese. My entrance caused a flurry of chatter and giggling among the younger girls, while the older women bowed and accepted me without so much as a raised eyebrow. They did, however, look me over.

I must admit that this first introduction to the institution of mixed bathing took a degree of courage I probably would not have had in my own country and culture. I knew mixed bathing was an accepted practice in Japan, and that my entering the bath was only unusual because I was a foreigner, not because I was a male. I knew there would be no objections or embarrassment on their part, and that whatever trepidations I felt were my own hangups—which I was determined to overcome.

After I had scrubbed and entered the pool, the older women immediately began trying to talk to me. Within a matter of seconds, I was completely at ease and relaxed. None of my earlier fears of sexual arousal and that sort of thing materialized. This is not to say, of course, that such things never happen or that they didn't happen on some other occasion, but my baptism was both painless and pleasurable, and I became a devotee.

You can make the transition from hungup neophyte to an experienced mixed-sex bather just as easily. It's all in your head, as the saying goes. The best time and place, as in my own case, is a hot-spring spa *(onsen)* where everyone goes knowing that "anything goes" at *onsen*. All you have to do is accept the fact that it doesn't make any real difference what strangers might think of you, that their opinions or judgments will not affect you in any way whatsoever.

The challenge is to come to terms with yourself; to accept yourself as you are without worrying about what others think. This, of course, is the message that psychiatrists preach to people having a wide variety of coping problems, particularly self-image and sex-related problems.

If you can accept yourself to the extent that you are not bothered at all by the thought or practice of mixed bathing, you are not likely to have any problems that would require psychiatric counseling. So put a hot-spring spa on your itinerary, and take the plunge.

CHAPTER X

Funiki Wo Suiageru
Soaking Up the Atmosphere

Strolling the Ginzas of Japan

Tokyo's *Ginza Dori* (gheen-zah doe-ree), which bisects the famous shopping and entertainment district known as "The Ginza," was the first street in Japan to be paved, the first to have Western-style streetlights, and the first to have buildings made of brick.

As a result of this early "international" development, Ginza Street became a magnet for Japanese and foreign residents alike before the end of the nineteenth century. Hundreds of thousands of people from Tokyo as well as adjoining cities and prefectures flocked to the Ginza on weekends and holidays to see the new Western-type buildings and streetlights, to shop for imported merchandise, and to eat and drink in the restaurants and bars that sprang up between the shops and department stores and on the backstreets of the area.

Ginza ni ikimasho! (gheen-zah nee e-kee-mah-show) or "Let's go to the Ginza," very quickly became one of the most commonly heard phrases in Tokyo. The custom of going to the Ginza just to stroll up and down the main thoroughfare and the backstreets became institutionalized as *Ginbura* (gheen-buu-rah) or "strolling the Ginza," and was something virtually everyone did on a regular basis well into the 1960s.

It used to be said that if you wanted to meet someone during this period—anyone, Japanese or foreign—all you had to do was go to the intersection of Ginza and Hibiya Streets (which used to be known as Owari-cho because laborers from the district of Owari were used to reclaim the land in the area), and wait. From 1952 until the early 1960s, the favorite rendezvous spot was the southwest corner in front of the Sanai Shop (now a high-rise building with a rounded front). While I waited there for a date one time in 1956, my high-school Latin teacher came by.

Really Old Japan Hands will recall that the Matsuya Department Store on the northeast corner of the Ginza-Hibiya Streets intersection was the main Tokyo PX during the American military occupation of Japan, and that one of the most popular GI hangouts in the city was the snack bar in the Wako Department Store on the northwest corner. Another flashback about this extraordinary era in U.S.-Japan relations: the Isetan Department Store in Shinjuku was used as billets by the Occupation forces. GIs by the hundreds used to sit on the brass rails that still ring the building and ogle the girls passing by.

Tokyo's Ginza was certainly not the only popular strolling street to develop in Tokyo or in Japan following the opening of the country to the West. It just happened to be the first one that was Westernized. In fact, "strolling streets" have been an integral part of Japanese life since the beginning of urbanization.

Many cities in Japan began as the sites of castles, temples, or shrines. There was always one main thoroughfare leading to the castle, the temple, or the shrine. Tradesmen invariably built their shops along these thoroughfares, since people going to and from the castles, etc., would pass by their storefronts. Virtually all traveling in Japan up to the 1860s and 1870s was by foot, so there was an almost constant stream of passersby.

All of the hundreds of post-station towns resulting from the institution of the "Processions of the Lords" (Chapter III) began as inns and shops lining both sides of the roads they were on, turning all of these "main avenues" into strolling streets.

Festivals and other festive occasions have traditionally been very common in Japan. Some were associated with shrines or temples, others with more commercial sponsorship. These events always attracted large numbers of people into the streets. Since Japanese homes have always been small and crowded, people spent a lot of time out in the streets, socializing and enjoying the pageantry of the passing crowds, with the great Processions of the Lords among the regular attractions during the long Tokugawa dynasty.

Japan's large cities today are made up of what used to be dozens of towns and villages that likewise grew up around shrines and temples, and in the case of Tokyo, around the mansions of the provincial feudal lords who were required to maintain their families in Edo during the last 247 years of the reign of the Tokugawa Shoguns. These former towns and villages are easily discernible in present-day Tokyo, Osaka, and other major cities in Japan. In Tokyo they include the well-known districts of Shinagawa, Akasaka, Ueno, Shinjuku, Nihonbashi, Ikebukuro, and so on.

The point is that each of these districts today has its own main thoroughfare and shopping/entertainment center where strolling remains a major form of recreation. Besides housewives walking or riding bikes to these shopping streets on a regular and often daily basis, families customarily take walks in their own neighborhoods on weekends and holidays—just to get out of the house and enjoy a bit of exercise and fresh air.

But the shopping, dining, and entertainment centers that have developed around important commuter transportation terminals in Japan's large cities remain the most popular strolling areas. Each of these areas is a microcosm of Japan—filled with humanity, jammed with every conceivable kind of retail store, restaurant, and night-spot, and ablaze at night with a jungle of neon signs that turn the areas into fantasylands.

Getting Off the Tourist Trails

Decades ago when I worked for the Japan Travel Bureau, I learned that the best way to ensure that visitors had a good time while they were in Japan was to take them into the backstreets of one or more of these shopping-entertainment districts and simply let them walk around and absorb the sights and sounds, stopping at places that caught their eyes, and letting them take time to investigate, to satisfy their curiosity.

I found that just one or two hours is not enough to get the full impact of this kind of experience. It requires a whole evening, say from 7 to 11 P.M. or later, depending on the age and stamina of the visitors. The idea is to go slow, look at everything, stop around 7:30 for dinner, go somewhere else for dessert, a third place for coffee, and then continue the stroll.

Around 10:30, again depending on the age and proclivities of the visitors, many choose to stop in briefly at one or more nightspots, which include bars, beer gardens, nightclubs, and cabarets.

Japan's thousands of cabarets are special in that they

employ large numbers of attractive female hostesses to sit with, cater to, and otherwise entertain male customers. Foreign women occasionally go to cabarets with male escorts, but they are designed for and almost exclusively reserved for men. (See Chapter XI, "Pleasures of the Night.")

Finally, one of the best ways to close out a night of getting acquainted with this side of the "real Japan" is to stop at a *yatai* (yah-tie), or street vendor, selling various kinds of snack food. Among the popular dishes available at *yatai* are *oden* (oh-dane), a kind of stew that includes vegetables and seafood; *okonomi-yaki* (oh-koe-no-me-yah-kee), a kind of egg-and-vegetable pancake, and baked sweet potatoes.

Some of these wheeled *yatai* food carts, particularly those selling oden, provide stools for five or six customers. The others are usually stand-up or take-away operations. *Yatai* selling hot food are especially popular during the colder winter season, and mostly come out at night in the entertainment districts. In summer, *yatai* can be found during the day on weekends and holidays, as well as at night. Daytime *yatai* may offer anything from ice cream to *yaki-tori* (yah-kee-toe-ree) or tidbits of chicken barbecued on wooden skewers.

Mixing with the Natives

A great many professional people in the travel industry (as well as in academia, the government, and elsewhere) labor under the misconception that observing another society as an outsider is enough—that you really don't have to get down with the natives to understand and appreciate a culture. As you know by this time, I'm a firm believer in going native.

There are several aspects to a culture—spiritual, intellectual, emotional, physical, and so on. If you really want to absorb even a piece of foreign culture you have to experience it; you have to participate in the lifestyle of the people so that it becomes a part of you.

As a short-time visitor to Japan, you are naturally limited in what you can do and how long you can do it. But you can at least get a taste of Japanese culture by meeting as many people (other than tourist guides and hotel staff) as possible, and I propose that you program in one or more days to be devoted solely to meeting and communicating (to whatever degree possible) with ordinary Japanese.

You can do this with structured home-visits arranged by a Japanese travel agency. You can make an effort to get advance introductions to Japanese individuals, through business or social channels. You can ask for help from travel agents, airline or hotel staff, or tourist information centers operated by the Japan National Tourist Organization. They *will* be interested in what you want to do and *will* try to help you.

Many Japanese will enthusiastically go out of their way to have a chance to meet and spend a few to several hours with foreign visitors—either out of a pure sense of hospitality or because they want to expose themselves to foreigners, to practice their English, to demonstrate goodwill, and to help make sure the visitor gets a good impression of Japan.

The Japanese take these things personally and seriously. It is therefore not so far out to suggest that you *can* make contact with private individuals after you arrive in Japan. One of the connections that works especially well is through schools. If a school in your own area does not have any kind of relationship with Japanese schools, you can have someone in Japan call a nearby school and tell them you would like to visit the school in order to learn something about the Japanese educational system so you can share the knowledge with your own school system when you return home.

This invariably gets you the invitation you are seeking, and often is expanded into a major experience that goes beyond the first meeting. Such impromptu meetings have, in fact, led to student exchanges and family visits.

If you live in or near a city that has a sister-city relationship in Japan it is very easy to go through this connection to arrange private meetings with one or more Japanese families. If you are a member of the Kiwanis Club or the Lions Club or the Masons, these organizations have thousands of members in Japan who can be contacted through their international headquarters. Members of these clubs are especially interested in direct person-to-person contact with foreigners.

While much smaller and more exclusive, Japanese members of the Young Presidents Club are another connection that can be used. The YMCA and YWCA organizations are very active in Japan, and are also excellent contact points for individual programs during visits to Japan.

One technique more affluent visitors sometimes use is to hire vacationing students (who are studying English) to act as their guides and companions while they are in Japan. This can be a marvelous way to really get acquainted with a typical Japanese, and often to make a lifelong friend. (This approach doesn't have to be limited to the school vacation periods. Japanese university students are very casual about attending classes, having only to pass the periodic examinations.)

Visitors who come to Japan via one of the Japanese airlines can begin the process of learning about the people and culture by first interacting with the airline flight attendants en route, and with everyone else they meet in the process of traveling. (I have noticed over the years that most travelers, particularly those in groups, have a tendency to spend most of their time abroad talking with each other, often virtually ignoring the local scene. This is not the way to learn about a foreign country.)

You should begin to use your Japanese-language ability as early as possible and on every occasion that presents itself. This is another area in which Americans in particular are very weak. Many Americans live abroad for ten or more years and do not learn to speak the local language. There is no excuse for this kind of extreme provincialism—and the world can no longer afford to indulge this kind of cultural myopism.

In addition to the mutual responsibility people have to understand and communicate with each other, the simple fact is that is what makes traveling abroad both fun and educational.

CHAPTER XI

Yoru No Asobi
Pleasures of the Night

The "Hot" Water Business

Most visitors to Japan get just a glimpse of a side of Japanese life that is much more important to the understanding of the people (and a lot more interesting to learn) than what one might imagine. This other side of Japan—which the Japanese do not talk about but otherwise do not hide—is known in Japanese as *mizu shobai* (me-zoo show-bye), or "water business."*

While the *mizu shobai* originally included theatrical and other types of entertainment, it is now primarily used in reference to the huge world of bars, nightclubs, cabarets, soaplands (massage-bath houses), and sometimes to a special category of hotels known as "lovetels," which specialize in renting rooms by the hour (although all-night rates are available) to couples seeking a private place for a short time.

---

*For a detailed discussion of this fascinating side of life in Japan, see the author's *Japan at Night—A Guide to Leisure and Recreation in Japan* (Passport Books).

The size of Japan's nighttime entertainment industry is astounding to the newcomer. It is in fact one of the largest industries in the country, and plays a far more important role in the economy and society than similar businesses abroad. One of the major reasons for the importance of the *mizu shobai* in Japanese life is that entertaining friends or guests at home is very rare, and is mostly limited now to the few who have become Westernized, and have larger than usual homes.

The Japanese are frequently visited in their homes by relatives, but when it comes to friends and business associates, particularly where entertainment is concerned, virtually all such meetings take place in coffee shops, restaurants, hotels, bars, clubs, or cabarets.

Home entertainment did not develop in Japan because houses were very small, very fragile, and very cold in the winter. The only form of heat was small *hibachi* (he-bah-chee) charcoal braziers, set on the floor, or in a covered floor-pit that people sat around with their feet and legs under the cover). Private homes were also acutely susceptible to fires from the *hibachi* used for heating and cooking.

While Japanese homes and apartments built in recent decades are constructed of much sturdier materials that are far less susceptible to flames, and much more effective methods of heating are now commonplace, they are generally still so small that the only "public" area in a typical home is a "living room" that is often no more than ten by twelve feet, with a number of furnishings that further reduce the open space.

Another factor in the immense size and importance of the nightime entertainment trades is that social etiquette in Japan was traditionally very detailed and very strict. About the only time one could "dispense with etiquette" was when drinking, during which time almost any kind of behavior was acceptable. The *mizu shobai* thus served as a giant stress-remover for the Japanese, allowing them to throw off their inhibitions and relieve their frustrations.

Yet another important element in the *mizu shobai* today is that businessmen have developed the custom of wining and dining prospects and customers (and themselves) in the bars, clubs, and cabarets that make up the key parts of the industry. This practice is regular and systematic, and accounts for much of the billions of yen that annually changes hands between the business community and the *mizu shobai*.

The visitor to Japan must know about the *mizu shobai*, how it works and why it is important, in order to have any in-depth insight about the country. But learning about the *mizu shobai* can be both expensive and painful if you do not follow some basic guidelines.

Cabarets, patronized almost exclusively by businessmen on expense accounts, normally do not have set prices, and are very expensive. Foreign patrons of cabarets are either highly placed executives with substantial entertainment budgets, or the guests of Japanese business associates. There are, however, a collection of cabarets in Tokyo, Osaka, Kobe, and a few other cities that cater to foreign customers, with posted prices that are well below what is usually charged Japanese patrons. These cabarets advertise in the English-language guide-type publications available in these cities (*Tokyo Weekender, Tour Companion, Tokyo Journal* in Tokyo, *Kansai Time-Out* in the Osaka-Kobe-Kyoto area).

Generally speaking the foreign community in Japan patronizes the beer gardens, hotel lounges, bars, nightclubs (which have hostesses but do set and post prices), discos, pubs, and restaurants that have various forms of entertainment, including live shows. Some, of course, also frequent the notorious soaplands, where the services run the gamut in the sensual arena.

Visitors in Japan have no problem finding a wide variety

of nightspots to explore. There are more than twenty-five thousand in Tokyo alone. The Ginza district in downtown Tokyo boasts 3,200 of these *mizu shobai* bars and clubs (along with its department stores and hundreds of boutiques and restaurants), which employ approximately 36,000 hostesses to serve and otherwise cater to their male clientele.

The travel industry in Japan, particularly Japan Gray Line, offers nighttime entertainment tours that include one or more cabaret stops (where they have special set prices for the tours). This is the easiest and most economical way to experience the typical nightspot scene. Among the half dozen night tours Japan Gray Line runs in Tokyo is one that includes a sukiyaki dinner, a geisha party, and a nightclub show. Another version of this tour offers a kabuki show in place of the nightclub stop.

The visitor to Japan generally will not go too far wrong by patronizing the nightspots that advertise in the English-language press. They are seeking foreign clientele, almost always operate under a Western system of pricing and paying, and can also be expected to have English-speaking staff or hostesses.

It is generally only the exclusive Japanese-style hostess places (whether they are called clubs or cabarets) that do not follow the Western pricing system, so one can usually go into any other kind of club or bar without worrying about being ripped off.

The Real World of the Geisha

There are perhaps half a dozen Japanese words known to most educated foreigners around the world. One of these words is *geisha* (gay-e-shah), which means "skilled person"—in this case women skilled in playing traditional Japanese musical instruments, in Japanese-style dancing, singing, and in catering to men more or less as personal waitresses and companions during eating and drinking parties.

Geisha have a long and mostly honorable history in Japan, going back several hundred years. The institution developed during the early decades of the Tokugawa Shogunate (1603–1868). During the first generations, the women were basically prostitutes, but as the practice grew into a profession, the status of the women went up.

Eventually the training of the geisha, along with their constant exposure to businessmen, political leaders, and the other elite of the country, made them into the best-educated, most experienced, and often most talented women in the country.

By the time internal and external pressures were undermining the long reign of the Tokugawa shoguns in the early part of the 1800s, the more talented and ambitious geisha themselves were high on the social scale in Japan. Famous geisha were ardently courted by leading businessmen and politicians, and often became their wives.

One young imperial prince fell in love with a geisha who already had a patron, and ended up having to borrow the money (from a madam in the *mizu shobai*) to ransom her. The young prince, who then married the geisha, was Hirobumi Ito, who went on to become one of the leading Japanese statesmen of his times, with a career that spanned more than fifty years.

With the downfall of the Tokugawa Shogunate in 1867–68, the status of the geisha lost some of its luster—primarily because the Japanese quickly learned that Westerners hid their extramarital affairs from public view, and that women of the pleasure world were looked down on. In their rush to emulate Westerners, the Japanese began to be more discreet about their recreational activities in the "willow world."

The profession of the geisha did not die, however, and despite having shrunk considerably in postwar Japan (because of competition from hostesses in cabarets, along with other forms of nightlife), it survives and thrives today in a pattern that has changed very little since Tokugawa days.

Perhaps the biggest change in the geisha world is that the cost of their services has become so high that only very successful businessmen and the highest-ranking bureaucrats and political officials (who are authorized to spend tax money on their entertainment) can afford them. The host of an evening that includes geisha can expect to pay anywhere from a thousand dollars—for a very small, very short party—to ten thousand dollars or more.

Much to the surprise and possible disappointment of many foreigners, the "geisha house" in the sense meant is a figment of their imagination. Except in outlying provincial areas, geisha generally do not live and work on the same premises. They live in apartments or other accommodations, and work in *ryotei* (rio-tay), which are inn-restaurants. The *ryotei* call them in when they have booked a party that wants the services of the geisha.

In earlier years it was common to see geisha being transported to and from *ryotei* in jinrikisha (generally lacquered black), but one is lucky to see this sight more than a few times a year now.

The *ryotei* utilizing the services of geisha are almost always clustered in areas that are known as "geisha districts." Among the more famous of these districts in Tokyo today are Akasaka, Shimbashi, and Yanagibashi. The Akasaka area, just down a hill from Japan's Diet Building and other government offices, is favored by the political leaders of the country.

Geisha *ryotei* do not cater to the general public. They are available only by reservation, and most of them require recommendations from known patrons before they will accept reservations. Parties are served in private Japanese-style rooms. Most of guests leave the *ryotei* at the end of the evening, but overnight lodging can be provided for those who desire it.

With few exceptions, the only foreigners who go to geisha *ryotei* today are the guests of Japanese hosts. There are several dozen inn-type restaurants in Tokyo, Osaka, Kyoto, and elsewhere which cater to foreign clientele and have "geisha" waitresses. Few if any of these *geisha* are members of the Geisha Association and they are unlikely to have gone through the professional training required by the association of members in good standing.

Of course, the foreign visitor generally cannot tell the difference between a professional licensed *geisha* and one who is unlicensed and lacks the traditional training. These "amateur" *geisha* can invariably sing and dance and often play the *shamisen* (sha-me-sane) as well. Virtually every Japanese girl-woman in the country knows how to interact well enough with male guests to satisfy that requirement.

If you want the genuine *geisha* experience, you need a guarantor and a fat wallet. I recommend you settle for cabaret hostesses. They are almost always far more attractive than *geisha*, cost far less, and you can have a lot more fun with them. The other choice is to patronize one of the foreign-oriented inn-restaurants that provide unlicensed *geisha* for their guests. See the local English-language guide publications for names and addresses of these establishments.

CHAPTER XII

Shoppingu-No Charenji!
The Shopping Challenge!

Strategies for Smart Shopping

Shopping has traditionally been one of the major attractions of foreign travel because it provides an opportunity for the ultimate consumer to cut out some of the middlemen and get much closer—if not directly—to the source of many popular, sought-after products, with substantial savings in cost.

The cost benefit is no longer a primary consideration in shopping in Japan, however. In fact there are many Japanese-made products that can be bought at cheaper prices abroad than they can in Japan itself. The reason for this is the current high disparity between the relative value of Japanese yen versus the dollar and other foreign currencies.

The cost of pearls, high-tech electronics, cameras, lenses, and other Japanese-made items that are now popular around the world has not changed significantly as far as their yen price is concerned, but the price of *yen* has more than doubled in recent years.

When yen was pegged at 360 per dollar, a ¥36,000 string

141

of pearls was a bargain at $100. Now that same string of pearls costs well over $200. Again, the price of the pearls was not raised. The cost of yen went up.

The disparity between the yen and the U.S. dollar is now such that many prices in Japan are simply outrageous from the American viewpoint. A cup of coffee, for example, ranges from $3 to $5. In a hotel, a glass of orange juice ranges from $4 to $6. An American-style breakfast in a hotel (which was $5 to $10 dollars until the mid-1980s), now costs from $15 to $30. These same extremes apply across the board when one converts dollars or some other weak currency to yen, whether we're talking about something to eat, wear, or enjoy.

There are, however, many ways to avoid these price extremes while in Japan, especially where food prices are concerned, and still be able to satisfy the urge to bring back gifts and souvenirs of the trip. Of course, you will have to go out of your way to achieve these savings because you will not find budget prices in hotels.

Where dining is concerned, the secret is simply to eat in ordinary Japanese restaurants, particularly those that feature set breakfasts, lunches, and dinners, which usually cost less than half of what you pay when ordering à la carte or in hotel restaurants.

Another gambit is to stop in at neighborhood markets and buy a two- or three-day supply of fresh fruits and possibly other items as well. Tangerines, apples, pears— especially the *niju-seki nashi* (nee-juu-say-kee nah-she) or "twentieth century pears"—persimmons, and bananas make excellent snacks. Eating an inexpensive and delicious tangerine (*mikan* / mee-kahn) is certainly an excellent substitute for a $4 or $5 glass of orange juice.

It is easy enough to go even further in saving on your food bills, if you are willing to do a bit of additional shopping. Western-style lunch meats, condiments, and a variety of outstanding breads are available in Japanese supermarkets, providing all the makings needed for a good old-fashioned sandwich.

Hotel Shopping Arcades

All of the luxury-class and most of the first-class hotels in Japan have shopping arcades on the premises—some of them with as many as two dozen or more stores, offering a variety of the products for which Japan is famous.

The prices in these shops are generally higher than those located outside of hotels simply because of the cost of the space. Furthermore, hotel arcade shops generally do not offer discounts or bargains of any kind. Their biggest attraction is that they save the shopper a lot of time and inconvenience because you can commute to and from them by elevator. They also offer a fairly large selection of the most popular gift and souvenir items under one very comfortable roof. If this convenience outweighs the cost factor, shopping for most of the things you might want to buy in Japan is very easy indeed.

The Tax-Free Shops

Several hundred shops in Japan, congregated in airports and downtown locations, are licensed by the government to sell tax-free gift and souvenir items to visitors and non-Japanese residents in possession of passports. The original purpose of the shops was to offer a price advantage to tourists to encourage shopping.

Tax-free shops still offer savings of ten to twenty percent off the regular retail price of various kinds of merchandise, particularly items classified in the luxury class. Another advantage of shopping at tax-free stores is that they stock a number of items that are popular with foreign visitors, have staff who speak English, and usually offer packing and shipping services.

But tax-free shops are few in number, and offer only a limited selection of merchandise, much of which is likely to be the same made-in-Japan products that can be bought abroad for less money. The best approach is to patronize these shops *when* they are convenient and when you have no better option, such as discount shops or discount districts where the prices are often substantially lower than those in tax-free outlets.

Discount Shopping

Discount shopping has always been popular in Japan but is even more extensive today because prices in Japan are high by any standards (in this case, in relation to how much the Japanese earn). In addition to regular bargain days and special sales at specialty stores, variety stores, and department stores, there are year-around discount shops and shopping areas in Tokyo and other cities that are known by virtually every Japanese.

The largest and most famous of these areas is the *Akihabara* (ah-kee-hah-bah-rah) district in Tokyo, a few minutes from the downtown area, where household appliances, electrical items and components, and a wide variety of electronic products are the main attractions.

Prices in Akihabara range from twenty to fifty percent or more below retail prices in regular stores, but because of the yen-dollar disparity, they are often not bargains for visitors. Often, now, only hard-to-find electrical or electronic parts are actually price bargains in Japan.

Reordering Your Shopping Priorities

The best approach to shopping in Japan today is to shop only for things not readily available abroad, such as specialty handicraft items, including such traditional things as garden lanterns (in metal or stone), interior decoration items such as *andon*-style lighting fixtures, a style of chinaware that is especially attractive, or art objects and other unusual items with a value (to you) that is not specifically related to their dollar cost.

All of Japan's prefectures and many of its cities have what is referred to as *meibutsu* (may-e-boot-sue) or "famous products," meaning products that have been made in their area for generations and are representative of the district. These products range from folding fans, teapots, wooden dolls, lacquerware, particular kinds of pottery and stoneware to bamboo utensils. (See Chapter 13 for a more complete listing.)

These local famous products, which are representative of traditional Japan and often not exported, make the best kind of gift and souvenir, since they are distinctive as well as rare. Among them are things that you can treasure for a lifetime. If you are going to be traveling to various cities and prefectures in Japan, you should take advantage of the opportunity to check out their *meibutsu*. The prices are generally much lower there than they are in tourist shops in Tokyo or Kyoto, for example.

The main point is that Japan is no longer the place to shop for strictly utilitarian products or equipment, and that the only real bargains in Japan today are traditional products that have intangible value. If you make up your shopping list with this in mind, you are much less likely to be disappointed with either prices or what you end up buying.

CHAPTER XIII

Mingeihin
Souvenirs with Soul

The Master-Apprentice System

Like many cultures around the world, the early industrial civilization of Japan was based on the production of tools, utensils, and other necessities by individuals who developed their skills to a high degree and then passed them on to assistants or apprentices.

In Japan the master-apprentice system was institutionalized in the society at a very early stage of its development, but masters from Korea and China also played a major role in the final flowering of the process. Beginning in the fifth century A.D. skilled craftsmen coming to Japan from the mainland changed from an occasional occurrence to commonplace, resulting in a renaissance of development in virtually every field of human endeavor.

Prior to these early contacts with the Asian mainland, Japan had no system of writing. Culture and civilization were transmitted by word of mouth, example, and on-the-job training. The Korean and Chinese masters who came into Japan had also been trained in the master-apprentice system, and found fertile ground for their knowledge and skills among the Japanese.

By the eighth century, the Japanese had imported and synthesized virtually the whole gamut of Chinese culture, adapting it to fit their distinctive philosophy. The output of the thousands of masters and skilled apprentices turned the lifestyle of the ruling class in Japan into a highly sophisticated existence that equaled or surpassed that in any of the great civilizations of Asia or Europe.

As this system continued for generation after generation, and the years of apprenticeship increased to decades instead of years, the level of skill required to achieve journeyman status became higher and higher, and eventually virtually every master craftsman was an artist. The finest craftsmen were master artists whose work achieved a classic style and beauty that today would win them fame and fortune—yet their work was so commonplace that only fairly affluent people could afford to buy it for ordinary use in their homes without attributing any special significance to it.

The poorest farmers and townspeople used pottery, lacquerware, and other handcrafted items that were the products of a proud tradition of quality that extended down to the lowest level.

When the first Japanese-made handicrafts reached Europe in the sixteenth century, their classic style and beauty made a tremendous impression on royalty and gentry alike. Many products that were simple kitchen utensils in Japan became treasured collectors' items to their new owners.

Much of the charm of modern Japan is bound up in the traditional products still being produced today by its master craftsmen, and Japan owes much of its popularity as a travel country to the men and women who have carried on the skills of their distant ancestors.

Further, the high standards of design and quality that are characteristic of most of Japan's contemporary high-tech products, from portable tape recorders and video cameras to cosmetics and watches, have their antecedents in the handicraft traditions of the past—and are now formidable factors in the efforts of American and European manufacturers to sell their goods in Japan.

These same traditions are responsible for the extraordinary inroads Japanese designers are making in the international fashion world, and are very likely to carry them to the forefront of this multibillion-dollar-a-year industry.

Because of significant differences in climate, in the availability of raw materials, and in the particular occupations that developed in early Japan, regions developed different product specialties. Farmers in the northern snowbound regions of the Tohoku district, noted since prehistoric times for its beautiful forests, became carvers of distinctive wooden dolls called *kokeshi* (koe-kay-she).

Iron ore was also found in surface deposits in the Tohoku region. Craftsmen in this area become known for their superb cast-iron bells and teapots. By the middle years of the long Tokugawa Shogun dynasty (1603–1868), virtually every region and province in Japan had its noted *meibutsu* (may-e-boot-sue) or "famous products," and travelers visiting these areas made a special point of buying them.

The Famous Things

Here is a selected list of the most famous products of some of Japan's leading city areas:

Tokyo: woodblock prints, toys, fans, cameras, electronic items, silverware, books, cloisonné, brocades, handmade paper, and pearls.

Kyoto: silk brocades from the Nishijin district, lacquerware, screens, dolls, scrolls, antiques, woodblock prints, damascene, cloisonné, and curios.

Osaka: silks, toys, antiques, art, and curios.

Kobe: bambooware, tortoiseshell ware, silk, and silk goods.

Nagoya: lacquerware, porcelain, chinaware, fans, cloisonné, and curios.

Kanazawa: kutani-yaki porcelains, silk, dolls, and lacquerware.

Nikko: woodenware, lacquerware, and curios.

Timeless Treasures

As we learned earlier, the pleasure trades in Japan are known as *mizu shobai* (me-zoo show-by) or "water business." I like to think that part of the reason for this unusual name is that pleasure is an ephemeral thing that evaporates like water—and the higher the climax of pleasure the more rapidly it fades after the peak.

Since a trip abroad is something like the "water business," in that the pleasures fade quickly once you return home, it is very important to acquire a number of tangible, permanent reminders of your trip—besides photographs.

The best kind of timeless treasures to take home from Japan are examples of its handicraft arts. I recommend a few choice ceramic, pottery, or lacquerware pieces that you thereafter keep as decorations, to be placed on a stand or shelf (the Western version of the *tokonoma*), where they can be seen and enjoyed for the rest of your life. Of course, hanging scrolls, Hakata dolls, kokeshi dolls, ironware, etc., can also serve the same purpose.

In addition, I suggest that you buy some lacquerware and chinaware for regular use (especially when you have visitors). Both wares are very distinctive and add a special allure to any setting. You will also be directly reminded again and again of your experiences in Japan. The memories will remain alive, and just as the tea host reserves the last measure of pleasure for himself, you will be able to make your memories of Japan a permanent part of your life.

Sayonara
("If It Must Be So")

It is easy to determine if people really enjoyed a visit to Japan. All you have to do is ask them, just before they leave, if circumstances permitted would they readily extend their visit by several days, and would they like to come back and stay longer the next time.

The answers you get are revealing about the travelers as well as about the efficiency and effectiveness of the travel industry. Travelers who are very positive about their experiences, and are enthusiastic about returning to Japan at the first opportunity, frequently express regret, however . . . about what they failed to do. Their biggest complaint is that they spent too much time sightseeing in "old Japan," and not enough time getting acquainted with the Japan of today, particularly the people.

If you have followed most of the advice in this book, that is much less likely to happen to you, and the Japanese word of farewell, *sayonara* (sah-yoe-nah-rah), literally "if it must be so," will have new meaning.

Your new familiarity with the language, the food, the customs, and the lifestyles of Japan will also add a new dimension to your everyday affairs, and the memories will stay with you for life.